IRISH
RAILWAYS

PAST and PRESENT

Volume I

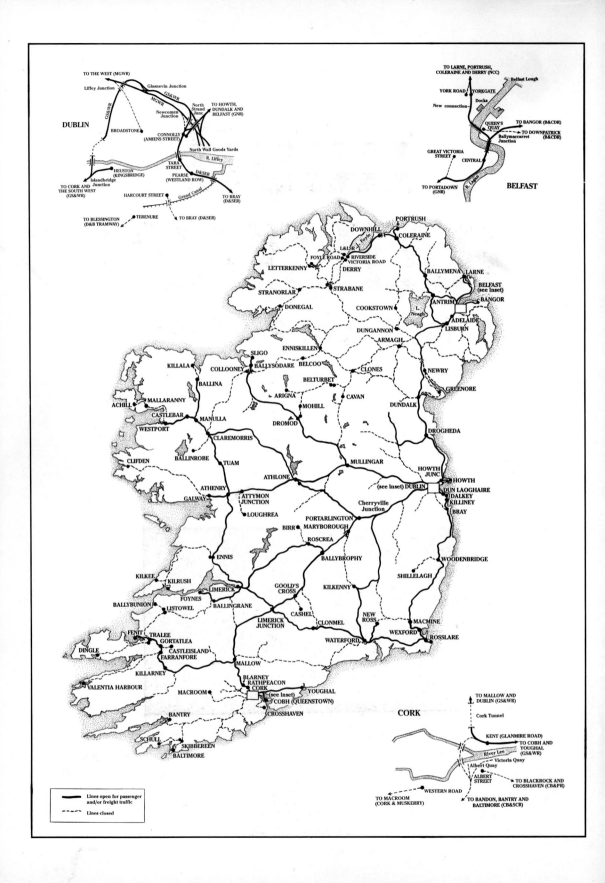

IRISH RAILWAYS

PAST and PRESENT
Volume I

Michael H. C. Baker

Past and Present

Past & Present Publishing Ltd

First published in May 1995
Reprinted December 1995

British Library Cataloguing in Publication Data

A catalogue record for this book is available from the British Library

ISBN 1 85895 046 5

Past & Present Publishing Ltd
Unit 5
Home Farm Close
Church Street
Wadenhoe
Peterborough PE8 5TE
Tel/fax (01832) 720440

Maps drawn by Christina Siviter

Printed and bound in Great Britain

MALLOW in the 1920s, with Aspinall 'D17' No 4 in charge of the Killarney branch train. The GS&WR, GSR and CIE certainly got their money out of this rather delicate-looking 4-4-0 - built at Inchicore in 1888, it survived for 69 years, being withdrawn in 1957. Note the cattle trucks in the sidings.

On 15 August 1993 the distinctive awning supports remain, but the milk churns have been replaced by litter bins and a palm, the cattle trucks by containers, and air-conditioned carriages of a Cork to Dublin express stand opposite where the wooden-bodied bogies waited nearly 70 years earlier. *Author's collection/MHCB*

CONTENTS

BANTRY was the most westerly station in County Cork, on the edge of Bantry Bay. It's difficult to date this picture, there being no rolling-stock in sight, but as there is no sign of activity around the shed in the foreground it may be after diesel railcars had taken over in the 1950s.

The tide is out but the town looks little different on 18 August 1993, although the track and buildings have vanished, the travellers' caravan standing more or less where the main station building used to be. The turntable pit remains, to the right of my wife, Maeve. I'm particularly fond of this picture, for I took it on our 25th wedding anniversary. *Author's collection/MHCB*

INTRODUCTION

This is really the story of a journey through Ireland, from the furthest east to the furthest west, and from north to south, which I undertook in the summer of 1993. Inevitably much of it was done by car - I was, after all, visiting many parts where the train had long ceased to run - but a good deal was done by train, too, diesel, electric and steam, standard (or should it be broad?) gauge and a tiny but significant bit of narrow gauge.

My long-suffering wife, Maeve, accompanied me, but justly complained that she had been driven through the Kingdom of Kerry, home of her ancestors, at such a rate that we had had no time to visit any of her relations. To remedy this we went back in the following spring, and I used the opportunity to repeat one or two pictures and capture the few locations that I had missed the previous summer.

This time we were accompanied by her parents, and I dedicate this volume to them in gratitude for their patience over the years, for allowing me to find the rotting remains of a Lough Swilly 'PD2' in a field near Malin Head, for crossing the Shannon to spend 10 minutes admiring the old West Clare station at Kilrush, and for all the diversions we have made together, without complaint - the quickest route from Dublin to Killarney is not via Mullingar. . . It was also jolly thoughtful of them to name their youngest daughter after Ireland's finest steam engine.

Although a number of pieces of the Irish railway system fell by the wayside before the Second World War, notably much narrow-gauge mileage, it was the 1950s and '60s that saw the real onslaught. This happened both north and south of the border. Much of it was inevitable, given the often pretty minimal service enjoyed by branch lines serving scantily populated rural areas that could be better served by the car, the lorry and the occasional bus. The Beddy Report of 1957, commissioned by the Dublin Government, recommended that the existing route mileage of 1,918 be halved and no fewer than 317 of the then current 373 stations and halts be closed. This was murder on a massive scale. In the North the picture was even gloomier, with the Benson Report of 1963 recommending that only the Dublin to Belfast, Belfast to Larne, and Belfast to Bangor lines remain.

In the event administrations in the South and North were not quite as ruthless as they promised, but it was a close-run thing, particularly in the Six Counties, where it really did seem at one time as though railways might disappear altogether.

Gradually, as the realisation dawned on the Western World that it could not go on indulging every whim of the motor car indefinitely, so in Ireland the railway began to inch its way back into favour. Was it not a rather good thing environmentally, did it not get people from their homes in the ever-growing suburbs to their places of work in the city and back out again more efficiently than any other means of transport, and was not the really up-to-date, air-conditioned train just about the most comfortable way of getting about the country?

Then again, as bright paint and hanging flower baskets, interpretative centres and folk museums transformed what had sometimes been rather shabby little towns and villages, often set in the most glorious scenery, into self-confident communities, worth visiting in their own right, so an old station, or, even more ambitiously, a stretch of long-abandoned railway, came to be seen as part of the community's heritage and history, worth preserving and, perhaps, reviving. Thus the seemingly gone-for-ever narrow gauge is making a modest return, while steam trains pop up and visit all sorts of unexpected places.

No praise can be too great for the Railway Preservation Society of Ireland. Founded in the early 1960s in the North, while others up there set about creating death and destruction, the

RPSI showed that a united interest in preserving something of the nation's transport heritage could transcend political, religious and historical divisions. As a consequence the achievements of what has always been a very small number of active participants have ensured the survival in working order of a wonderful collection of locomotives and carriages unique within the British Isles. RPSI trains have travelled the length and breadth of the 26 counties, and the Society's pioneer work has inspired others so that the preservation movement, whether it be of rolling-stock, stations, stretches of line or many other artefacts, is flourishing - if hardly financially over-endowed - in a manner wonderful to see.

Michael H. C. Baker
Wareham, Dorset

DUBLIN CONNOLLY (AMIENS STREET): Following the 1925 amalgamation, trains from the Midland Great Western main line were diverted from Broadstone station, Dublin, to the former D&SER side of Amiens Street station and on to Westland Row (later Pearse), where they terminated. Maunsell-designed 'K1a' 2-6-0 No 396 is seen entering Amiens Street with the up Galway day mail in June 1951. *David Murray*

Forty-two years later another 2-6-0 pulls into Connolly station. To commemorate the 50th anniversary of the 1916 uprising, Amiens Street was renamed after James Connolly, the great trade union leader who was executed for his part in the event. Former D&SER 2-6-0 No 461 has charge of the empty stock of the RPSI Dublin-based train of mainly former CIE corridors, about to load up and set off for Rosslare Harbour. *MCHB*

Rosslare to Dublin

ROSSLARE: Our story begins down in the far south-east at Rosslare. The railway reached this rather barren, featureless stretch of coastline in 1882, but its days of glory arrived in 1906 when the Great Southern & Western Railway of Ireland and the English (and Welsh) Great Western opened the mail boat service between Fishguard and Rosslare. This was all part of the GWR's great decade of expansion, when it determined to wrest some of the lucrative Irish Sea traffic from its London & North Western rival. New lines were built on both sides of the Irish Sea and the boat trains to and from Rosslare ran by way of Waterford, Dungarvan and Mallow to Cork, with connections thence to the transatlantic port of Queenstown. In this picture, taken in 1976, a General Motors '141' Class Bo-Bo diesel-electric of CIE stands beside the sea wall, preparatory to running round and taking out the boat train for Waterford, Limerick Junction and Limerick (the Dungarvan line having been closed in 1967). Opposite is the Sealink ferry preparing to sail for Fishguard.

The 2 August 1993 view is from the deck of the Fishguard ferry *Stena Felicity*, tying up at the same spot as in the previous picture, after a somewhat bumpy ride from Fishguard. Again a '141' Class has charge of the connecting boat train from Limerick, while approaching the harbour is the B&I ferry *Isle of Innisfree* from Roscoff. *Both MHCB*

ROSSLARE MPD on 26 April 1955. In front of the shed is No 310, a 'D10' Class 4-4-0 built by the GS&WR in 1903, while alongside on the turntable road - the turntable is hidden behind the shed - is Woolwich 2-6-0 No 384. Its designer, R. E. L. Maunsell, had once been CME of the GS&WR, but these 'Moguls' did not appear until he had moved to the South Eastern & Chatham Railway and were actually constructed at Woolwich Arsenal for the 1914-18 war effort. They were sold in kit form to Ireland after the war and were the mainstay of the Rosslare boat trains from the 1920s until displaced by dieselisation a year or so after this picture was taken.

The shed now belongs to ship repairers, but the line to the turntable remains in use and on it on 21 August 1993 stands another 'Mogul'. This is No 461, one of two powerful inside-cylinder engines built by Beyer Peacock for the Dublin & South Eastern Railway in 1922. No 461's principal duty was on the heavy night goods between Rosslare, Wexford and Dublin, although the pair also put in much work on heavy passenger excursions. Withdrawn in 1965, No 461 eventually passed to the Railway Preservation Society of Ireland who restored it to working order at their Whitehead headquarters in Northern Ireland. Since then it has returned to its old stamping grounds, being based in Dublin. *H. C. Casserley/MHCB*

Above WEXFORD: The line from Rosslare to Dublin is a most attractive one, not least the section where it passes along the quay at Wexford. Watched by a group of sea salts, No 44, an ancient McDonnell express engine, built for the GS&WR in 1878 and an example of Ireland's first 4-4-0, heads south in about 1930.

Some 40 years later, in the summer of 1970 a train of Rosslare-bound diesel-hauled post-war CIE carriages heads past a lightship towards the location of the previous picture. *P. Ransome-Wallis/MHCB*

Right Finally we see the same location from the window of a passing train in August 1993. *MHCB*

Above WOODENBRIDGE in 1950: 44 miles from Dublin and 48 from Wexford, this was the junction for the Shillelagh branch until it was closed in 1944. The 6.45 am from Rosslare Harbour to Dublin, headed by impatient GS&WR-built 'D4' Class 4-4-0 No 335, waits to get the road once the down train, the 7.25 am from Dublin to Rosslare, headed by 'J15' Class 0-6-0 No 172, has arrived in the station.

On 21 August 1993 no trace of the station remains, only the single-track main line. This picture was taken from the Rosslare to Dublin 'Seabreeze', hauled by former Dublin & South Eastern 2-6-0 No 461, seen a moment ago at Rosslare. *Seaton Phillips/MHCB*

Left On the same day No 461 is seen once again about to set off from Greystones for Rosslare Harbour. *MHCB*

BRAY: The arrival of the railway in Bray, 14 miles south of Dublin, in 1854, turned it into the country's principal seaside resort. A Dublin to Greystones train pulls out of the station in August 1976; the shed is occupied by a diesel railcar. The single track of the line to Greystones, Wexford and Rosslare can be seen disappearing into the distance beyond the shed and curving towards the sea to take on the   spectacular climb around the foot of Bray Head.

The 06.57 Arklow to Dublin and Drogheda, hauled by a General Motors '141' Class Bo-Bo, pulls into Bray in August 1993. If I had taken this picture from the footbridge, as was the case with the 1976 one, all that would be in view would be a shimmering sea of electric overhead. The transformation of the Dublin suburban scene between Bray and Howth by the inauguration of the electrified Dublin Area Rapid Transportation (DART) on 23 July 1984 was quite astonishing. On the first Sunday of the service the *Irish Times* said that the route was 'busier than any day since the line opened in 1834', and the Journal of the Irish Railway Record Society spoke of 'the almost constant continuous procession of trains between Howth and Bray.' Here two DARTs stand in the now roofless depot, waiting to follow out the diesel-hauled Drogheda train. *Both MHCB*

KILLINEY (1): A five-coach train, headed by '670' Class 0-6-2T No 672, drifts around Killiney Bay in about 1956. Five of these engines were built by the Great Southern Railway in 1933 for suburban work in Dublin, one of the very few new designs turned out by that impoverished company. All disappeared in 1959, except for No 673, which lasted until 1962. The leading carriage is a new 10 ft 2 in wide, lightweight, 82-seat Park Royal, while the rest are much older, narrower, wooden-bodied vehicles.

In the 'present' view a DART passes the same spot on 30 March 1994. *Author's collection/MHCB*

KILLINEY (2): As the AEC-engined Park Royal railcars introduced by CIE in 1951 wore out, they were converted from 1972 onwards into push-pull units for the Dublin suburban services. One such train, of five cars, stands at Killiney station in August 1975 bound for Bray in the charge of B202, one of the smaller brothers of the '001s'. This was originally a Crossley-engined Metro-Vickers 550 hp Bo-Bo introduced in 1956. As such the Class was an almost complete failure, being both underpowered and totally unreliable. Fuel pipes constantly broke and they often produced more smoke - though a lot less power - than a steam engine. They were rebuilt with General Motors 1,040 hp power units from 1969, and from then became useful members of society.

The section of line between Killiney and Dalkey is probably the most photographed in Ireland. On one side is the sea, on the other some of the most desirable property in the country. The Greek-temple-like building with the pillars set on the hillside belongs to Bono of U2, 'The World's Most Famous Pop Group'. Bernard Shaw lived a bit further up the road, numerous other famous artists and writers, including James Joyce, have also had homes in the vicinity, and there are a number of embassies set amongst the trees of Killiney Hill. If I was offered my choice of any residence I have ever seen I would have 'Strawberry Hill', a wonderful late Victorian house on Killiney Hill with unrestricted views across the Bay, and diesel, electric and the occasional steam trains running along the bottom of the garden. It is not fanciful to compare Killiney with the French Riviera. A DART pulls out of the station in August 1993. *Both MHCB*

DALKEY station on 26 April 1955. This was originally the terminus of an atmospheric railway that opened in 1844, and so took the fancy of I. K. Brunel, who came over to take a look, that he persuaded the GWR Directors to let him build one in South Devon. Both lines were failures and the Dalkey line was converted to conventional haulage in 1854; there is an 'Atmospheric Road' in Dalkey to commemorate it. In this picture CIE No 466, a 4-6-0T of the Cork, Bandon & South Coast Railway, is running around its train (note the guard with his lamp). The CB&SCR possessed a number of engines with this unusual wheel arrangement; they mostly stayed on their home territory after amalgamation, but No 466 worked Dublin suburban trains for a number of years and was well liked by her crews.

A DART at Dalkey in March 1993; my wife, Maeve, stands in place of the guard on the repaved platform. A new, higher footbridge has been installed to clear the overhead wires. Dalkey station is always beautifully kept, enhanced with many flowers and much greenery. *H. C. Casserley/MHCB*

DUN LAOGHAIRE PIER: *Top* Carlisle Pier on 5 July 1960. Built 101 years earlier, when it was known as Kingstown, this was the principal port for Wales and England. Just arrived from Holyhead is the MV *Hibernia*. This motor vessel of around 5,000 tons was ordered by the LMS in 1946 from Harland & Wolff of Belfast and delivered in July 1948, the largest and fastest British cross-channel ship - along with her sister *Cambria* - of her time.

About to set off for Dublin is 'J15' Class 0-6-0 No 184. The 'J15s', or '101s', are Ireland's most famous steam engines. Introduced by the GS&WR in 1866, 119 were built between then and 1903, making them easily the most numerous class in the country. Described by Jack O'Neill, a Waterford driver who knew them well, as 'great and versatile', they worked every sort of train, and lasted until the end of steam on CIE. Two, including No 184, have been preserved. *F. W. Goudie*

Middle General Motors 950 hp Bo-Bo No 175 leaves Carlisle Pier for Heuston station, Dublin, on 26 August 1980. Alongside the pier is the MV *St Columba*, the 1977 car ferry replacement for the *Hibernia* and *Cambria*. I once spent 14 hours instead of the usual three aboard the *St Columba* - it was Christmas-time and a gale that began to blow while we were crossing from Holyhead became so intense that at times the wind was gusting at force 12 (so the captain informed us), making it impossible to dock at Dun Laoghaire. We spent the night pitching and tossing up and down the Irish coast and eventually staggered in around breakfast time. The most respectable people had long since lost all sense of dignity and were laying about on the decks, devoutly wishing that the ship would sink and bring their miseries to an end. *MHCB*

Bottom With the DART electrification the Carlisle Pier line closed. Rumour had it that it might either re-open, or a travolator be installed. Neither came about - instead passengers have since had to make do with a substitute bus, ill-equipped to cope with the large amounts of luggage always carried. In this August 1993 picture, a Bus Eireann single-decker stands where the trains once waited, while cars come off the now renamed and repainted *Stena Columba*. *MHCB*

DUN LAOGHAIRE: In 1952 No 334, a '321' Class 4-4-0 built by the GS&WR, has charge of a Dublin to Rosslare train on the main line. At this time there was only one platform here, a most inconvenient arrangement for this busy station, 6 miles from Westland Row, Dublin, used by commuters and day-trippers as well as boat trains to and from the Pier station. *Author's collection*

By August 1993 the DART electrification had utterly transformed commuter travel along the shores of Dublin Bay. A second platform had been added some years earlier, and a frequent regular-interval service carries huge numbers of travellers. Long-distance services to Wexford and Rosslare still operate through Dun Laoghaire. *MHCB*

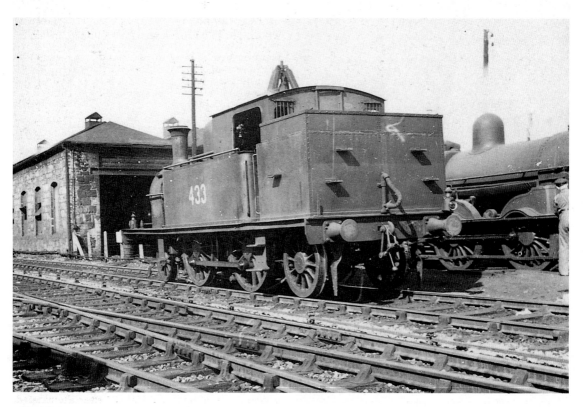

Dublin

GRAND CANAL STREET DEPOT, with 2-4-2T No 433 outside, in about 1953. This engine was actually built at Grand Canal Street, which was part of the Dublin, Wicklow & Wexford Railway's works. It first saw the light of day as 2-4-0T No 46 *Princess Mary* in 1888, being rebuilt in 1910. Its various owners certainly got their money's worth, for it was not withdrawn until 1957.

Seeming little changed externally in this March 1994 picture, No 433's birthplace now rejoices in the title of Barrow Street Chief Engineer's Plant Depot. *Kevin Murray/MHCB*

PEARSE (WESTLAND ROW): Bo-Bo No 206 enters Dublin Pearse with a Howth to Bray push-pull on 14 August 1980. Originally known as Westland Row, this was the terminus of Ireland's first railway, the Dublin & Kingstown, opened in 1834. It became a through station in 1891 and was renamed Pearse, after one of the leaders of the 1916 uprising, Padraic Pearse, during the 50th anniversary commemorations in 1966.

A Howth to Bray DART enters Pearse in August 1993. The 19th-century school buildings outside the station in Westland Row have been replaced by something a good deal more delicate and rather better illuminated. Immediately behind is Trinity College. I can never enter Pearse station without thinking of *Educating Rita* - the Michael Caine film of Willy Russell's play, which made Julie Walters and the Open University famous, was filmed here, in Trinity College and in the nearby streets, a number of early post-war CIE carriages being repainted in BR grey and blue livery to give the illusion of the UK mainland. *MHCB*

TARA STREET: The loop line connecting Pearse and Connolly stations runs through, or rather above, the very heart of Dublin on an elevated section of track that takes trains past the edge of Trinity College, through Tara Street station, over the Liffey, a couple of blocks from the Abbey Theatre, around the back of the Custom House, past Busaras (Central Bus Station), the Bridewell police station and into Connolly station. In this view, taken from the roof of Liberty Hall, the headquarters of the trades union movement and the highest building in Dublin, a Bray-bound commuter train pulls out of Tara Street on a sunny summer evening in 1969.

The same view in August 1993 shows DARTs leaving and approaching Tara Street station. *Both MHCB*

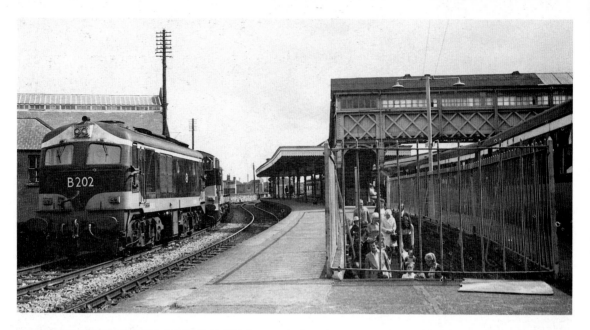

CONNOLLY (AMIENS STREET, D&SER) (1): The former Amiens Street station was originally two separate stations, the through D&SER one, and the GNR terminus, side by side. In this 1975 view of the former D&SER section, commuters descend to street level from a Bray to Howth push-pull, while B202, coupled to a GM '121' Class Bo-Bo, stands on the through road.

The same spot in August 1993 shows that, with electrification, the through side of Connolly station was completely rebuilt. Commuters head up and down a slope replacing the steps, while one of the latest type of push-pull units, No 6102, composed of modified BR Mark IIIs and dating from 1989, waits to depart for Maynooth, a suburban service introduced in 1981. *Both MHCB*

CONNOLLY (AMIENS STREET, D&SER) (2): Christmas Eve, 1979 - a picture taken from the 10.27 Dalkey to Howth train in the former D&SER station. Through the pillars the 11.00 'Enterprise' express for Belfast, unusually composed of an NIR '80' Class DEMU, can be seen pulling out past the locomotive depot.

In August 1993 an Irish Rail modified BR Mark III push-pull set stands at the same platform, the 1980s supports and awning contrasting with the ornate 19th-century ones. *Both MHCB*

CONNOLLY (AMIENS STREET, GNR) (1): The 2.30 pm to Belfast Great Victoria Street pulls out of Amiens Street in June 1951. The locomotive is No 87 *Kestrel*, one of the Glover three-cylinder compounds of 1932. An ancient six-wheel item of rolling-stock can be seen over No 97's buffer beam, while a 1915-built 'U' Class 4-4-0 waits to back out after the express has departed.

The 'present' view shows Irish Rail 2,250 hp Co-Co No 078 about to depart from Dublin Connolly with the 07.55 to Belfast Central in August 1993. *David Murray/MHCB*

CONNOLLY (AMIENS STREET, GNR) (2): Connolly at dawn on 31 December 1979. A thick frost covers the sleepers, and to the left, in the former GNR terminus, stand two General Motors Bo-Bos and two Metro-Vickers 'A' Class Co-Cos, while over in the through former Dublin & South Eastern section is a push-pull unit and another GM. The signal box at the end of the through platforms was built by the Great Southern Railway in 1934 when colour light signalling was introduced.

The 'past' picture was taken from the steps of the now demolished former GNR signal box, so this one, at dusk on 21 August 1993, had to be taken from ground level. A '121' Class Bo-Bo stands on the far left, but the centre of attraction is former D&SER 2-6-0 No 461 on the far right, just arrived from Rosslare with an RPSI special. *Both MHCB*

CONNOLLY (AMIENS STREET, GNR) (3): A view towards the GNR signal box at Amiens Street station in 1949, taken looking through the cab of railcar D, built by the GNR in 1936. A 'T2' 4-4-2T is approaching; on the right is the engine shed.

The bay platform from which the previous picture was taken was filled in when the DARTs were introduced. This picture was taken from the cab of an Irish Rail '121' Class Bo-Bo at the opposite platform face. CTC signalling, remotely controlled from the centre at Connolly, has meant the disappearance of the manual boxes in the area. The engine shed, still used by diesels and the occasional steam engine, is obscured by the dismally ugly carriage servicing depot, erected by CIE in the 1970s. *Seaton Phillips/MHCB*

BROADSTONE, the Midland Great Western Railway's Dublin terminus, on 18 July 1934. 'J10' 0-6-0T No 614, dating from 1891, performs station pilot duties, not a very arduous task in a station where hours would pass in perfect stillness. Broadstone closed in January 1937, services being diverted to the more central Amiens Street, although the locomotive depot remained open for over 20 years.

Broadstone in April 1993 has long the home of the provincial bus fleet, yet it is astonishing how little it has changed. Both the buildings seen in the previous picture, the stone one to the left and the pitch roof over the platforms, remain, as does the magnificent stone exterior and colonnade. *H. C. Casserley/MHCB*

LIFFEY JUNCTION: A train from Galway, hauled by two '141' Class GMs, takes the line for Glasnevin Junction (see page 39) and Connolly in August 1970. The lines to the left of the picture lead down to Broadstone station, although they were only in use for a few hundred yards, the rest being overgrown with weeds, prams and super-market trolleys. The station had long fallen out of passenger use, but the sidings were used for stabling wagons, often on their way to Mullingar for breaking up.

By August 1993 the signal box from which the previous picture was taken had been demolished, hence the lower viewpoint. All the sidings have gone, but a bit of the one-time Broadstone route, disconnected, remains, while a new station, through which a train from Sligo, hauled by a '121' Class GM, is passing, has been newly opened at Broombridge. *Both MHCB*

HARCOURT STREET: As well as the coast line to Westland Row, the Dublin & South Eastern Railway had a second route into the centre of Dublin via the 9-mile branch from Shanganagh Junction, 1 mile north of Bray, which headed through the suburbs of Foxrock and Dundrum to its Harcourt Street terminus, a few hundred yards' walk from St Stephen's Green and very nearly as close to Dublin's other university, University College, as was the Westland Row line to Trinity. Despite this, patronage rather fell away in the 1950s and the decision was taken to close it. No 2652, one of the 1954-built suburban AEC/Park Royal diesel railcars, stands at the single platform on the last day of operation, 31 December 1958.

No sooner was the Harcourt Street line closed and the track removed than the realisation began to dawn that this was all rather a mistake. The roads leading into the city from the suburbs that the Harcourt Street line had served grew ever more congested as the suburbs themselves grew. Eventually, rather too late, a ban was put on any further building over the trackbed, and various proposals were made to re-instate the trains. This being easier said than done, discussion has now gone on for over 35 years. However, some form of replacement looks increasingly likely, hopefully light rail, which would not actually use the old Harcourt Street terminus but would take to the streets just before reaching it and thus bring the tram back to the heart of Dublin.

The handsome facade is intact and used as offices, and this view, from approximately the same position as the previous one, shows that the roof remains, the trackbed has been filled in to platform level, and several dividing walls have been put in. This section is used as a garage. *Author's collection/MHCB*

TERENURE: A steam tram of the Dublin & Blessington Tramway at Terenure, the city terminus, on 17 August 1929. Terenure was not *very* city, being distinctly outer suburb in 1929. The 15-mile-long line ran to Blessington, at the foot of the Dublin Mountains, and was popular with day trippers.

The tramway closed on 31 December 1932, and buses took over; Dublin City double-deckers still run, but right through from the city centre to Blessington today. This is Terenure in August 1993. *H. C. Casserley/MHCB*

HEUSTON (KINGSBRIDGE) (1) is the headquarters of Irish Rail. This is the arrival platform in August 1972, and Co-Co A56R, a Metropolitan-Vickers locomotive of 1955, rebuilt with a 1,500 hp General Motors power unit in 1970, has just arrived with an express from Cork. Erected in 1844, Kingsbridge, as it was known until 1966, has a magnificent exterior, but its interior is far less impressive, and for most of its career could boast only one arrival and one departure platform, with a bay let into the latter.

The same location in August 1994 shows General Motors Co-Co No 86 having just arrived. Built in 1976, these 18 2,450 hp locomotives hauled the principal passenger trains on CIE and Irish Rail until the advent of the '201' Class in the summer of 1994. Heuston station is busier now than at any time in its history, with extra platforms and serving not only the Waterford, Cork, Tralee and Limerick lines, but also the former Midland destinations of Galway, Westport and Ballina. *Both MHCB*

HEUSTON (KINGSBRIDGE) (2): No 62 (*left*) fills the Edwardian sky as it heaves its train of four- and six-wheelers out of Kingsbridge in the early years of the century. No 62, a '60' Class 4-4-0 built in 1891, was designed by Ivatt, who later went to the English Great Northern Railway. The train standing alongside is at the Military platform, so called because it was often used for troop trains bound for the Curragh camp.

In the second view we see in the same position No 59, a member of the immediately preceding '52' (CIE 'D17') Class, which was designed by Aspinall, who, like Ivatt, would become famous in England for his 'Atlantics', in this case on the Lancashire & Yorkshire Railway. The loco is in charge of a Tullow branch train immediately after the Second World War.

In the 'present' view General Motors Co-Co No 078 pulls out of Heuston with a Cork express in August 1993. Remarkably the double-post telegraph pole on the right is still in place. *National Railway Museum, York/P. Ransome-Wallis/MHCB*

HEUSTON (KINGSBRIDGE) (3): '101' Class 0-6-0 No 132 shunts three gaunt-looking horse boxes and a six-wheel 3rd in about 1910. Built in 1888 and rebuilt into the form seen here in 1909, No 132 served the GS&WR, the GSR and CIE for 77 years.

Over 80 years later, in August 1993, '071' Class GM No 075 backs down on to its train. A generating car for air-conditioned stock is the nearest vehicle in the carriage sidings, and beyond is the RPSI train of preserved vehicles of early post-war CIE stock. *National Railway Museum, York/MHCB*

HEUSTON (KINGSBRIDGE) (4), and a deceptively archaic-looking view. It purports to be London Bridge station in the 1850s, the engine a 2-2-2 and the carriages a Dover boat train. Thus were Heuston station and '101' Class 0-6-0 No 184 disguised for the Sean Connery/Donald Sutherland film *The First Great Train Robbery* in 1978.

The same viewpoint in April 1994 sees No 075 just arrived from Waterford. The station roof, which dates from the 1840s, is instantly recognisable in both pictures, but how skilfully the film-makers disguised everything else! *Both MHCB*

Dublin to Waterford and Cork

DUBLIN CONNOLLY (AMIENS STREET): No 801 *Macha* pulls out of Amiens Street, as it was then, with the 10 am Cork Mail on 16 April 1948. Although the three magnificent 'B1a' sisters had little chance to show their paces before the austerity years of the Second World War clamped down on the Great Southern, and recovery afterwards was very slow, they were still highly thought of when this picture was taken. Reputed to be the fastest of the three, just how fast *Macha* was is recorded by W. McDonnell in *A Decade of Steam*. 'Loco 801 was for a time fitted with a speedometer . . . this apparatus folded up registering 103 mph.' *Macha* was withdrawn and broken up in 1962, but her sister, No 800 *Maeve*, can be seen in the new Transport Museum at Cultra, Northern Ireland.

The 'A' Class Metropolitan-Vickers Co-Cos brought the days of the 800s' preeminence to an end. Re-engined No A41R is seen at the same spot with a empty stock train in August 1969, consisting of two arc-roofed brake vans, built by the GS&WR in 1912, a post-war composite, and No 351, the GS&WR Royal Saloon of 1902, later the State Saloon, and still in existence today, although in a derelict condition, at Inchicore. *H. C. Casserley/MHCB*

GLASNEVIN JUNCTION in March 1971, and No B114, one of the two pioneer CIE main-line diesels, is heading a transfer freight from Heuston to North Wall. B113 and 114, 960 hp Sulzer-engined Bo-Bo diesel-electric locomotives, were built at Inchicore in 1951. They originally worked main-line passenger trains between Dublin and Cork, but in their later years they were mostly confined to freight workings such as the one depicted here. Both locomotives still exist, although in a very dilapidated state, at Inchicore, and B114 is seen there (*centre*) in August 1993. Glasnevin is a double junction on the line that links all the Dublin passenger stations and goods depots. B114 is skirting the wall of

Glasnevin cemetery on the former GS&WR line from Islandbridge, and is heading for North Strand Junction, where the lines to Connolly and North Wall diverge. In the foreground is the line linking this with the former MGWR main line to Liffey Junction (page 30), Maynooth and the west.

On 6 August 1993 the Fridays-only 17.05 Connolly to Sligo passes Glasnevin Junction. It is crossing from the former GS&WR line to join the MGWR line, which runs parallel to it from North Wall and Connolly. The latter is much less well used than the former, and the MGWR connection to Connolly via Newcomen Junction was removed early in 1994. The crowded 17.05, powered by two '141' Class GMs, is composed of Cravens, the oldest carriages in regular main-line use on Irish Rail, built between 1961 and 1967. *All MHCB*

ISLANDBRIDGE JUNCTION in about 1932, with a heavy Dublin to Cork express double-headed by two former GS&WR engines, No 311, a 4-4-0 dating from 1903, and a '400' Class 4-6-0 of 1916-22. Designed by E. A. Watson, who had come to Inchicore from Swindon, the '400s', although big and handsome, were far from successful and they were all rebuilt or scrapped from 1929 onwards. The train engine is either No 401 or 406, both of which were drastically rebuilt with Caprotti valve gear in 1930. The fourth coach is one of four Pullmans introduced by the GSR in 1926. The line from Glasnevin Junction can be seen curving in at the extreme left of the picture, and the train is climbing the bank from Kingsbridge (later Heuston) station.

In August 1993 General Motors 2,250 hp Co-Co No 080 of 1976 pulls out with a Heuston to Cork express composed of BR Mark III stock modified by CIE with 'plug' doors. Kingsbridge was renamed after Sean Heuston during the 1966 commemorations. *Author's collection/MHCB*

INCHICORE: A sequence of down expresses on the main line at Inchicore between 1936 and 1994.

In the first picture No 403, one of the '400' Class built as four-cylinder engines by Armstrong Whitworth in 1922 and rebuilt at Inchicore with two cylinders in 1933, poses - for I don't think it is moving - with the Cork Mail composed of new steel-sided stock in 1936.

The next picture, taken in about 1949 features once again No 801 *Macha*, one of the three magnificent 4-6-0s, the finest of all Irish passenger engine classes, built at Inchicore in 1939/40. She is once again in charge of the Cork Mail, but this time the stock is vastly more varied, ranging from turn-of-the-century, wooden-bodied carriages, through a Pullman to a couple of new post-war steel-sided composites. Terraced houses occupy what in pre-war days was fields on the other side of the tracks.

The third view shows a couple of veteran 4-4-0s in charge of another motley rake on Sunday 13 June 1954. The pilot is Ivatt-designed 'D14' No 86 of 1886, the train engine Coey 'D2' No 321 of 1904. Both were scrapped in 1957.

The fourth picture brings us into the diesel era with No A22R, one of the Metropolitan Vickers 'A' Class Co-Cos of 1955-7 that swept away so much CIE main-line steam, and were later rebuilt with General Motors 1,250 hp power units. A22R accelerates south-westwards with a nine-coach Cork express composed of post-war steel-sided carriages in August 1973. It is passing a pair of arc-roofed GS&WR Edwardian corridor carriages used on the Inchicore works train.

Finally we see General Motors 2,250 hp Co-Co No 083 of 1976 with air-conditioned BR Mark III stock forming the 09.00 Heuston to Tralee on Tuesday 29 March 1994. In the siding is an engineers ballast train. *Author's collection/ E. M. Patterson/P. Ward/MHCB (2)*

INCHICORE WORKS: In August 1970 No C227, one of the underpowered 550 hp Metro-Vickers Sulzer-engined Bo-Bos, heads a line of locomotives awaiting a new lease of life with General Motors power units.

In August 1993 No 128, one of the original General Motors single-cab Bo-Bos of 1961, stands in the same location at the head of a line of withdrawn '001' Class Co-Cos.

By contrast, in another part of the Works rakes of newly delivered Japanese Tokyu Car Co-built diesel railcars await entry into service on the new Dublin-Kildare and other expanding suburban routes in March 1994. *All MHCB*

44

INCHICORE SHED: On 24 April 1955 a fascinating collection of locomotives stands in front of CIE's largest depot at the very end of the era when steam was, if not supreme - for the diesel railcars were much in evidence - then at least in the ascendancy. Among the classes on view are several of the inevitable '101s', Woolwich and 'K3' 'Moguls', a 'D4' 4-4-0, and a 'J13' 0-6-0T.

In August 1972 there is nothing but diesels as far as the eye can see. These include an '001' (formerly 'A' Class), 130 hp 'G' Class Deutz four-wheelers of 1955/62, three Birmingham Sulzer 'B101' Class 960 hp A1A-A1As of 1956, a former GNR BUT railcar, and CIE/Maybach 400 hp diesel-hydraulic shunters of 1955. All have now vanished.

In August 1993 there is a simplified track layout and fewer locomotives, with General Motors '121' and '141' Class Bo-Bos and '001s' in evidence. *H. C. Casserley/MHCB (2)*

CHERRYVILLE JUNCTION is 32 miles down the main line from Heuston.

In the first picture No 321, the pioneer member of its class, built at Inchicore in 1904, hurries the two-coach 6.00 pm Dublin to Waterford via Carlow train past the junction in August 1955. *David Murray*

Looking in the opposite direction, this August 1975 picture shows James Bond's favourite locomotive passing the distinctive-looking signal box with a Dublin-bound express. The turn-out for the Waterford line has now been reduced to a single track. *MHCB*

In March 1994 two General Motors Bo-Bos head out of the setting sun with an up tanker train. The signal box remains, but is no longer used as such with the advent of CTC. Note the tall signalling mast standing in front of the box. *MHCB*

46

WATERFORD (1): *Jumbo* shunting at Waterford in about 1920. Originating in 1877, this GS&WR 0-6-0T shows no sign of its number, 201. The tank loco wheel arrangement, so common in England, Wales and Ireland, was relatively rare in Ireland, reflecting the lack of demand for shunting engines. Nevertheless *Jumbo* had an extraordinarily long life, not being withdrawn until 1963.

No 143, a CIE '141' Class General Motors 875 hp Bo-Bo, shunts at Waterford on 28 March 1994. *Author's collection/ MHCB*

WATERFORD (2): A freightliner pulls out of Waterford for Dublin in August 1976. Waterford is the home of Belferry, a firm whose containers are a familiar sight on both sides of the Irish Sea and which provides Irish Rail with a large volume of traffic. Nowadays most containers travel on bogie wagons, and guard's vans have been abolished.

The 10.50 express for Dublin Heuston pulls out of Waterford on 28 March 1994. Semaphore signals are still a prominent feature of the Waterford scene. *Both MHCB*

WATERFORD (3): The east end of the station in August 1976 sees General Motors Bo-Bo No B147 having just detached itself from its train from Dublin while another member of the Class in later livery stands on one of the through tracks with the lightweight goods train from New Ross.

On 28 March 1994 General Motors 2,250 hp Co-Co No 083 stands at Waterford with the 11.35 from Heuston. There has been no regular traffic over the New Ross branch, which once linked up with the Dublin to Wexford and Rosslare line at Macmine Junction, for several years now. *Both MHCB*

BALLYBROPHY (1): No 401 passing Ballybrophy, 66 miles from Dublin, with the Cork to Belfast 'Enterprise' on 25 October 1952. This interesting train ran for a short while in the early 1950s, linking Ireland's three principal cities, but demand was insufficient to sustain it and by 1956 the Dublin-Cork and the Dublin-Belfast 'Enterprise' expresses had reverted to running as separate trains. The stock here is provided by the GNR.

The substantial stone buildings on the up platform remain on 15 August 1993, as does the footbridge; however, all that remains of the signal box on the down platform is its reinforced concrete base. *David Murray/MHCB*

BALLYBROPHY (2): No 801 *Macha* speeds through Ballybrophy with the 10.30 Kingsbridge to Cork express in September, 1955; 38 years later, on Sunday 15 August 1993, No 078 passes with the 08.50 Heuston to Cork express.
David Murray/MHCB

BIRR: Former GS&WR 0-4-4T No 295 of 1895 stands at Birr at the end of the branch from Roscrea on the Ballybrophy to Limerick line on 24 April 1953.

Birr station is now a private residence, as seen here on 18 August 1993. The Birr branch closed on the last day of 1962. *H. C. Casserley/MHCB*

CASHEL: A train headed by a 'J15' ('101') Class 0-6-0 and a 'D14' 4-4-0 pulls out of Cashel in the summer of 1953.
Cashel, with its beautifully restored castle, is one of the most historic sites in Ireland, and receives many visitors, being conveniently placed on the Dublin to Cork main road. Unfortunately it was a lot less convenient for rail travellers, being at the end of a branch line from Goold's Cross, between Ballybrophy and Limerick Junction on the Dublin-Cork main line, and it closed in September 1954. A mare and foal stand on the site of the sidings in this August 1993 picture. *Author's collection/MHCB*

LIMERICK JUNCTION (1) has long been a bit of a joke, chiefly on account of its eccentric track layout, but also because it's a fair way from Limerick, 22 miles to be precise, but not a very long way from Tipperary, 2 miles distant. Situated on the main line from Dublin to Cork, and the junction of lines to Limerick and Waterford, until 1967 up and down main line trains could only reach the lone, very long, through platform by reversing. In this 22 April 1955 view looking south, the train on the right is standing in one of the bay platforms, bound for Limerick and in the charge of No 306, a 'D12' 4-4-0 designed by Coey of the GS&WR in 1902. On the left is a down main line train, headed by another 'D12' and about to perform the complicated square dance that will bring it alongside the platform.

On Tuesday 5 April 1994 the 09.00 Cork to Dublin train, made up of air-conditioned BR-built Mark IIIs has arrived alongside the through platform in a conventional manner and will depart likewise. In the bay platform on the right is the 10.12 connecting train to Limerick, in the charge of GM Bo-Bo No 151. *H. C. Casserley/MHCB*

LIMERICK JUNCTION (2): Looking north now, on 22 June 1959 the 1.14 pm Dublin to Cork passenger train, headed by one of the 'A' Class Metro-Vick 1,200 hp Co-Cos in its original silver livery, stands at the platform, having reversed in from the down main line. In the distance can be seen the engine shed with smoke rising from some of the many steam engines still shedded there at that time.

The same location on 15 August 1993 sees a Metro-Vick Co-Co, long since re-engined by General Motors, shunting wagon loads of empty Guinness barrels. The division of the long platform into two sections remains, although reversal is no longer necessary. The station itself has been modernised and brightened. One wall of the engine shed remains. *D. Thompson/MHCB*

MALLOW is an important junction on the Dublin to Cork main line. This view was taken looking north from the down main line platform in the 1920s. The engine shed can be seen in the distance through the footbridge beyond the north end of the station.

In this view from the up side, a Dublin to Cork train headed by No 079, a General Motors 2,450 hp Co-Co diesel-electric, stands at the down main platform. On the up platform the distinctive ornate canopy remains, but Bermuda shorts and backpacks, not slightly below the knee skirts and cloche hats, are in fashion on 15 August, 1993. *Author's collection/MHCB*

BLARNEY: On 9 July 1934 GS&WR-built '**J15**' ('**101**') Class 0-6-0 No 193 arrives with a down train of six-wheelers.

The site of Blarney station on 15 August 1993 shows that the down platform has vanished and the up platform, seen on the left of the first picture, has been cut back. The station buildings have become a private residence. A returning GAA special, consisting of a push-pull set hauled by a '121' Class Bo-Bo, is approaching. The famous castle is down in the valley to the left of the picture. *H. C. Casserley/MHCB*

RATHPEACON, 4 miles out of Cork, is seen on a sunny summer afternoon around 1928, with a down express hauled by one of the handsome four-cylinder 4-6-0s designed at Inchicore by E. A. Watson in 1916. Sadly the ten engines of the Class fell well below expectations, and all were either withdrawn or rebuilt around 1930.

On 16 August 1993 the first down passenger train of the day, the Mondays-only 05.40 Dublin Heuston to Cork, hauled by '071' Class Co-Co No 076, speeds down the bank towards its destination. It was not possible to take the picture from precisely the same spot on the overbridge where Rex Murphy had stood, for foliage completely blocked the view, so I moved until I was standing over the up main line rather than the first siding. The sidings, where goods trains were marshalled, mostly remain, as does the signal box, but all have fallen out of use. *Rex Murphy/MHCB*

Cork

KENT (GLANMIRE ROAD) (1): The classic view of Cork Glanmire Road station, which was renamed Kent during the 1966 commemorations. The steep 2-mile-long bank out of the station at 1 in 78-64-60 necessitated double- and sometimes triple-heading in steam days. A 'D14' 4-4-0 and a 'B2' ('400') 4-6-0 prepare to set out with a Dublin express on 5 August 1949.

On 5 April 1994 General Motors '141' Class Bo-Bo No 152 stands on the spot occupied by the 'D14' some 45 years earlier, while the air-conditioned stock of a Dublin express occupies the other platform. *Author's collection/MHCB*

KENT (GLANMIRE ROAD) (2): 'B2a' ('400') class 4-6-0 No 402 sets out from Cork station, taking the avoiding line behind the passenger station, with the overnight Dublin goods in September 1959. A 'J15' Class 0-6-0 shunts cattle wagons in the sidings beside the docks.

    On 5 April 1994 a General Motors Bo-Bo stands on the avoiding line, now reduced to a single track. There are Harp lager wagons in the sidings, and a grain silo on the opposite side of the docks. *Both MHCB*

KENT (GLANMIRE ROAD) (3): 'J15' Class 0-6-0 No 182 stands in Cork station with a train from Mallow on 19 August 1953, while over four decades later, on 5 April 1994, General Motors Bo-Bo No 153 stands at the same spot, also with a train from Mallow. *A. David Parkes/MHCB*

CORK SHED in the early 1950s. 'B2a' Class No 406, one of the big express 4-6-0s rebuilt with Caprotti valve gear in 1930, is being prepared to take out a Dublin express, while in the background is a GS&WR-built 'F6' 2-4-2T of 1892-4.

Standing in front of the shed on 16 August 1993 is No 036, originally one of the 58 'A' Class Metro-Vickers Crossley-engined Co-Cos of 1955-7, rebuilt with General Motors power units from 1968. *J. D. Robertson/MHCB*

ALBERT QUAY: This was the approach to the quay in 1970. It was originally the terminus of the Cork, Bandon & South Coast Railway, and was connected to the GS&WR by a track that ran along the quays and through the city to Glanmire Road, but by this date the West Cork lines had all been taken up and Albert Quay was used for goods only.

When I tried to repeat this picture in 1993 I was at first completely foxed, for there seemed no point of reference, bar the houses in the distance on the hillside on the far bank of the River Lee. Then I found a couple of old telegraph poles and gradually worked out that the dual carriageway from which this picture is taken had been blasted through the rock cutting and built on the former trackbed, more or less wiping out all trace of where the railway once ran. *Both MHCB*

ALBERT STREET was the terminus of the narrow-gauge Cork, Blackrock & Passage Railway, and is seen here on 9 July 1934. Unlike the traditional image of the Irish narrow gauge, this line was almost suburban in character, serving as it did the south-western suburbs of the city and the west side of the harbour. It had closed in September 1932, nearly two years before this picture was taken.

The first picture was taken from a long-demolished footbridge, this 16 August 1993 one from a roundabout. At first glance I thought all evidence of the railway had been wiped out, although the rows of buildings on either side remain largely unaltered. However, further inspection revealed not only the telegraph pole, which is being passed by the donkey cart in the 1934 picture, but also the station building itself, its pitched roof visible over the hoarding for Careys tools. *H. C. Casserley/MHCB*

Past and Present
Colour

Ireland

DUBLIN CONNOLLY station, formerly Amiens Street, at dusk on 22 December 1981. The passenger walking away from the camera is standing on what used to be the edge of the Howth bay platform, then recently filled in. To the left are the through platforms of the once separate Dublin & South Eastern station, to the right the former Great Northern Railway's terminus.

On a bright March morning in 1994 we can see that the semaphore signals and signal box have gone. The former DSER station was completely rebuilt on the inauguration of the DART suburban electrics in 1983. In the former GNR station is an Irish Rail '121' Class diesel-electric, and, further down the line, a Northern Ireland Railways '111' Class Co-Co. *Both Michael Baker*

EAST WALL JUNCTION, DUBLIN: The Belfast-bound 'Enterprise', the 11.00 from Connolly, passes East Wall Junction in August 1969. The 'Enterprise' is the generic name for all through passenger expresses between the two capitals. The seven-coach train is headed by '70' Class diesel-electric railcar No 77, built three years earlier. These Ulster Transport Authority (UTA)-designed units had then recently taken over from GNR ones.

The 'Enterprise', now timed to leave Connolly' at 11.20, passes the same spot on 31 March 1994. The locomotive is No 113 *Belfast & County Down*, a 2,250 hp General Motors Co-Co diesel-electric, introduced by Northern Ireland Railways in 1984. The carriages are BR Mark IIb's and one Mark IIc, put into service at various dates from 1970 onwards; the livery dates from 1989. The tower of Connolly station and Liberty Hall, Dublin's highest building and the Trades Union headquarters, appear in both pictures, but the signal box and semaphores of 1969 have long gone, and the supports and overhead for the DART electrics are now prominent. Fluorescent jackets would not have been around in 1969. *Both Michael Baker*

HOWTH JUNCTION: A Drogheda-bound morning commuter push/pull train made up of converted Park Royal rail-cars, propelled by a 'B201' Class Bo-Bo diesel-electric, stands at the down main platform in December 1981. The tracks curving away from the junction are those of the Howth branch. Beyond are flats and houses dating from the expansion of the Dublin suburbs northwards in the post-war years and immortalised as Barrytown by Booker-Prize-winning author Roddy Doyle.

On 31 March 1994 a Dublin-bound suburban train composed of Craven carriages built between 1963 and 1967 stands at the up main line platform in the charge of a General Motors '141' Class Bo-Bo. Since electrification of the Howth branch it is no longer possible to exactly repeat the previous shot, for the sides of the footbridge from which it was taken have been raised and covered in. Gone are the palm trees, the semaphores and the signal box; the concrete suburbs beyond are unchanged. *Both Michael Baker*

DUN LAOGHAIRE PIER station on an August evening in 1979, with a 'B201' Class Bo-Bo, a Metro-Vickers design dating from 1957, re-engined by General Motors from 1970 onwards, about to depart for Pearse, Connolly and Heuston stations, Dublin, with a boat train. Standing alongside is the 7,839 gross ton Sealink ferry MV *St Columba*, dating from 1977.

The railway closed in 1980 and the track was taken up, leaving intending rail passengers either a long walk, laden with luggage, to the main-line station at Dun Laoghaire, or a ride on a double-deck bus, ill-equipped to carry luggage, to the city stations. On the evening of 28 March 1994 the ship is the same, but now renamed *Stena Hibernia*; it is due to be replaced by a vastly bigger ferry, but there is much controversy whether this should use an enlarged Dun Laoghaire Pier, disgorging more and more cars and juggernauts on to the town's inadequate road system, or be transferred to the North Wall, Dublin. *Both Michael Baker*

MULLINGAR: Moving west now, to the former Midland Great Western line from Dublin, we visit Mullingar on an icy cold December day in 1979. A '001' Class is about to depart with the 08.20 Dublin to Galway mail. Although a weak sun shone, the temperature remained below freezing point all day.

No trains are to be seen nowadays, for all Dublin to Galway and Westport services go by way of the former GSWR main line as far as Portarlington, and no regular traffic disturbs the rust-covered rails between Mullingar and Athlone. Otherwise, on 2 April 1994 nothing much seems to have changed; there is even a covering of white, a freakish spring snowstorm having just swept over the surprised inhabitants of Mullingar. Beyond the station at the junction with the Sligo line can be seen two carriages belonging to the Railway Preservation Society of Ireland (RPSI), which has its southern headquarters here. *Both Michael Baker*

LISTOWEL was on the former Limerick-Tralee line. Passenger services ceased in 1963, although an occasional freight or passenger special still passed this way when this photograph was taken in August 1978. The signal box, although boarded up, is intact; beyond are the station buildings and footbridge. The donkey is standing where the Listowel & Ballybunion monorail, which closed in 1924, used to curve in and run alongside the main-line station.

All that remained of Listowel station by 7 April 1994 was the ruined buildings on the down platform, the track having been lifted and the footbridge and signal box demolished - the frame can just be seen lying by the fence. I cannot say what happened to the donkey. *Both Michael Baker*

GLANMIRE ROAD, CORK: At the Cobh end of the station in August 1977 a Class '001' Co-Co is approaching with a freight from one of the yards further down the River Lee towards the open sea. A General Motors Bo-Bo is in the yard just behind the signal box, while beyond another '001' is just visible in front of the locomotive depot.

The same view in April 1994 shows that the signal box has been repainted and fitted with new windows, and all the nearer semaphores have been replaced by colour lights, although further on and down the Cobh they still flourish. The track layout has been simplified; on the far left stands an '071', while outside the depot are a couple of General Motors Bo-Bos. *Both Michael Baker*

BELFAST: Finally, Northern Ireland steam in service and in preservation. Former Belfast & County Down Railway 4-4-2T No 221 (UTA number) stands at Queens Quay, Belfast, after overhaul in 1953. No 221 was built by Beyer Peacock in 1921 and withdrawn in 1956.

An earlier example of the class has, however, been preserved. No 30, built by Beyer Peacock in 1901, is now to be seen in Belfast Transport Museum. *Colour-Rail/Michael Baker*

COBH (1), known as Queenstown until Eire became independent, used to be the last port of call for westbound transatlantic liners. At the time that this picture was taken, on 14 April 1955, Cunarders still regularly sailed in and out of Cork Harbour - tenders ferried passengers to and from the quayside. However, the principal traffic was local, and a fairly intensive service was operated between Cork city and the stations along the 11-mile line skirting the eastern shores of the harbour. Cobh is a prosperous, handsome little town, with a quite magnificent cathedral, dedicated to St Colman and designed by the younger Pugin. Its spire can be seen above the retaining wall directly above 'J15' 0-6-0 No 105, which is backing down on to its train, ready to set off for Cork.

Cobh is still entirely dependent upon the train for public transport, there being no bus service to Cork, and the railway is as busy as ever. The pioneer '141' Class GM 875 hp Bo-Bo backs on to its train on 17 August 1993. *H. C. Casserley/MHCB*

COBH (2): As befitted a transatlantic port Cobh had an impressive terminal building, through which passengers passed to board the liner tenders. A CIE Park Royal railcar, forming the 9.30 am from Cork, has just arrived on 20 June 1959.

With the end of the transatlantic traffic such lavish facilities were no longer needed. On 14 June 1993 a most imaginative transformation was unveiled by Albert Reynolds, the Prime Minister, when the Queenstown Story was ceremoniously opened. Within the terminal buildings the sometimes harrowing, constantly fascinating history of the millions of immigrants and others who sailed from Queenstown to a new life is told in a highly imaginative manner, from sailing-ship days through the heyday of the liner, the *Titanic* and *Lusitania* tragedies with which Queenstown was so intimately involved, down to the ocean-going salvage tugs of the present day. This is the Queenstown Story cafe in the former terminal buildings on 17 August 1993. *D. Thompson/MHCB*

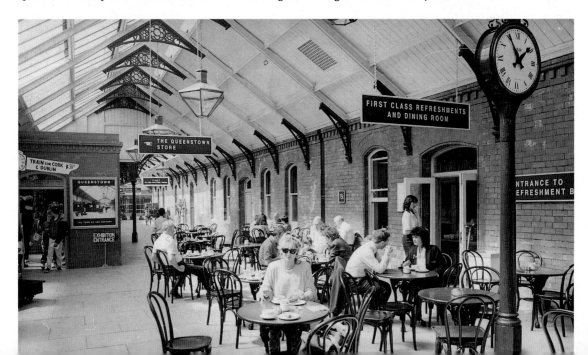

The South West: Cork to Tralee and Listowel

SKIBBEREEN in the 1930s. This is the Cork, Bandon & South Coast Railway station, opened in 1872, but basically dating from 1893 when the 8-mile extension to Baltimore was constructed, and closed, along with the entire former CB&SCR section, in March 1961. Skibbereen was also served by the Schull & Skibbereen 3-foot-gauge line, which opened in 1888, struggled on through the 1930s and the Second World War years and finally succumbed in February 1947.

On 17 August 1993 the signal box, now covered in ivy, remains, complete with chimney and slightly askew adjoining pole, while the station buildings have become part of Hurley's Jet Garage. Beyond, the narrow gauge station also survives with a surprisingly accurate painting of one of the Schull & Skibbereen Peckett 4-4-0Ts on one end. *Author's collection/MHCB*

VALENTIA HARBOUR was the most westerly railway terminus in Europe. On 14 April 1955 'J15' 0-6-0 No 127 has brought its train over the 39-mile branch from Farranfore on the Killarney to Tralee main line,. Even today Valentia seems a long way from Dublin. No through trains were ever normally worked to the capital, but in 1955 a GAA football special left Valentia at 10 pm and arrived in Dublin just in time for breakfast the next day, 9 hours 33 minutes later!

Little remains on 18 August 1993, but the low stone structure behind the derelict tractor upon which I am standing pinpoints the location. Behind the camera is the pier from which boats used to sail across to Valentia Island. The line closed in 1960 and nowadays a causeway, further up the coast, links the island with the mainland. All that remains of Valentia station is a crumbling little brick station house next to a fish factory. *R. M. Casserley/ Maeve Baker*

CASTLEISLAND: A General Motors Bo-Bo shunts at Castleisland in August 1974. The station was situated at the end of a 4-mile branch line from Gortatlea on the Killarney to Tralee line. Passenger traffic had ceased some time before I took this picture, yet the engine that originally operated the branch when it opened in 1875 is, remarkably, still in working order. This is No 90, the little 0-6-0T that lives at Tuam. It was built as part of a steam railmotor and converted to its present form some years later.

The Castleisland branch closed in 1977, and on 2 April 1994 the horse is standing approximately where the locomotive is in the first picture. A car park occupies the station site, behind the camera, while the iron gate beyond the horse leads to a water development scheme. *Both MHCB*

TRALEE (1): This is the north end of the station in August 1977. No 085 has just arrived with an express from Dublin, and beyond the gates the freight-only Fenit and Limerick lines cross Edward Street and continue through the goods yard, close by where the Tralee & Dingle narrow gauge line used to be.

On 17 August 1993 No 184 has just arrived with the 15.15 passenger train from Cork. The semaphore signals have gone and buffer stops prevent further progress, reinforced by an extension of the stone wall. The wooden level crossing gates have been replaced by smaller, metal ones for the remaining single track. *Both MHCB*

TRALEE (2): The goods yard is seen here from Rock Street crossing, looking towards the passenger station, in August 1974. In the foreground is the Fenit branch, running parallel to the North Kerry Limerick line.

The same view in August 1993 shows that the goods yard has quite disappeared, its site occupied by Dunne's supermarket beyond the wall on the right. The Fenit line remains, although long disused and invisible beneath the grass and the weeds. *Both MHCB*

DINGLE station was the terminus of the 3-foot-gauge line from Tralee. Standing in front of the shed on 14 July 1934 is No 5, a 2-6-2T built in Leeds by Hunslet in 1892, the year after the line opened. This 32-mile-long railway linked remote Dingle with Tralee and thus with the rest of Ireland. L. T. C. Rolt described it as 'the most remote and spectacular railway byway in the British Isles'. Dingle town depended upon its harbour for its existence, trading at different times in its history with Spain, whence it imported wine, America, whence it exported immigrants, and, latterly, fishing. Beyond Dingle town the peninsula was the most westerly point in Europe, the nearest parish to America. When the railway arrived almost all the inhabitants spoke Irish and even today, when the motor car has opened up the Dingle in a way the railway was never to achieve, there are still more Irish speakers here than anywhere else on the mainland. It is, perhaps, the most beautiful and most remote part of Ireland.

Cattle traffic kept the line open until 1953. Part of the station site is now the premises of O'Connors funeral parlour and motor company, the rest being occupied by Telecom Eireann. On 17 August 1993 the buildings remain,

and although the engine shed has gone, the water tower beside which No 5 was pictured in 1934 can still be seen, covered in foliage and partly hidden by the beer casks. When the line shut No 5 was transferred to the Cavan & Leitrim line and then, after that closed in 1959, Edgar T. Mead, a resident of New Hampshire, had it shipped to the USA, following in the footsteps of so many Dingle men and women. *H. C. Casserley/MHCB*

Above No 5 began a new life in preservation across the Atlantic, but there were those who always hoped the last surviving Tralee & Dingle locomotive might one day return to Ireland. The dream came true in 1985 when it was decided that the revival of the T&DR might be possible by incorporating it into the Blennerville windmill project. Blennerville was the first station out of Tralee, where the railway turned away from the estuary of the Lee and began its climb through the hills and mountains of the Dingle Peninsula. The windmill, which stood beside the estuary, was being restored to working order and it was decided to relay part of the line as far as Blennerville station, a few yards from the windmill. In 1992 No 5 steamed once again, and here it is on 18 August 1993 running around its train at Blennerville. *MHCB*

Right No 5 in charge of its two-coach train, imported from Spain, which runs every hour daily, crossing a tributary of the River Lee with the hills of the Dingle Peninsula in the distance. *MHCB*

LISTOWEL (1): This is the station in August 1969, with up and down freight trains passing. Listowel was the most important station on the 43-mile line from Limerick to Tralee, known as the North Kerry line. Regular passenger traffic ended in 1963. This is a view looking towards Tralee, and the up train is headed by Metro-Vickers rebuilt 'A' Class Co-Co No A38R.

All is ruin on 18 August 1993, the line having been abandoned in 1988. An elderly lady waited while I took this picture, then told me how sad she was to see such a state of affairs. 'My father was foreman here for 36 years. The Council took the bridge down and the itinerants did the rest.' *Both MHCB*

LISTOWEL (2): The Tralee end of the station, also in August 1969, with A38R shunting while a sister locomotive waits with the down train; the up and down daily trains always passed at Listowel. Beyond the signal box the Lartigue monorail ran into its terminus behind the GS&WR station.

The goods shed is the only structure still intact on 18 August 1993. *Both MHCB*

THE LISTOWEL & BALLYBUNION MONORAIL was, as has been said many times, a totally freakish contraption. The brainchild of a Spanish (or was he French?) engineer called Charles Lartigue, it opened in 1888, linking the seaside town of Ballybunion (population 373) with the market town of Listowel (population 2,965). It would have made a good deal more sense if it had been an ordinary narrow-gauge line, like so many similar lines then being built, but it wasn't. The locomotives were built by the long-established Leeds firm of Kitson, but there normality ended, for each of the three had two boilers and was of the utterly unique 0-3-0 wheel arrangement. Viewed side-on, the carriages, as this picture shows, looked relatively conventional, but this they were not, for they were built in two sections with the monorail running down the middle. Mobile steps were strategically placed in each train for passengers to cross from one side of the track to the other, as this group are doing. Judging by the fashions the picture must have been taken just before the line closed on 14 October 1924.

I had long known of the Lartigue for my wife's family comes from around Listowel, and my father-in-law remembers it well; many are the tales I have been regaled with over the years. What I never expected was to see a section of it restored. However, one should never underestimate a Kerryman. One summer Cousin Mick said, 'Come and see what Mickey Barry's got.' Michael Barry farms at Lisselton, midway between Listowel and Ballybunion, his land bordering where the monorail used to operate. Over the years he and neighbouring farmers had ploughed up bits of the track and trestles and he had painstakingly reassembled a section, plus a couple of running wheels, a lamp and several other relics, so that here, risen like a phoenix, is a reconstruction of the Listowel & Ballybunion monorail in Mickey Barry's farmyard.
National Railway Museum/MHCB

The West: Limerick, Galway, Athlone and Sligo

LIMERICK (1): CIE 'G3' Class 2-4-0 No 291, built by the Waterford, Limerick & Western Railway in 1893, at Limerick on 22 April 1955. One of only three types of 2-4-0 to survive long enough to appear in the 1949 edition of *The ABC of Irish Locomotives*, it lasted until 1959.

Irish Rail '141' Class Bo-Bo No 172 at Limerick on 9 April 1994. Although only colour lights are to be found in this part of the station, semaphores survive further out by the locomotive depot and works. *H. C. Casserley/MHCB*

LIMERICK (2): No 291 is seen again in this 16 April 1955 view, standing on one side of the signal box, while a couple of modern steel-bodied CIE-built carriages stand on the other. A cattle truck is prominent among the wagons in the sidings.

On 9 April 1994 we see that a concrete-sided signal box stands on the site of the former brick and wooden one. The lines curving out from under the end carriage in the 1955 picture, which took passenger trains on to the Foynes and North Kerry lines, have gone, passenger services having been withdrawn, although the Foynes line remains open for freight, reached by a junction half a mile out, at Limerick Check. A container depot occupies the goods sidings.

Ballingrane, some 17 miles from Limerick, used to be the junction of the Foynes and North Kerry branches. My mother-in-law, a native of Foynes, tells the story, which she swears is true, of a local man travelling on the last train of the day, slightly the worse for wear after considerable lifting of the elbow, who instructed the guard to put him out at Ballingrane, regardless of how difficult it might be to rouse him, in order to catch the connection to Foynes. Hours later the man woke up to find himself in Limerick. He gave the guard a fearful dressing down. The latter, eventually getting a word in, remarked: 'You can make as much noise as you like, it won't equal that of the fellow I put out at Ballingrane.' *H. C. Casserley/MHCB*

LIMERICK (3): In August 1975 a boat train for Limerick Junction, Waterford and Rosslare Harbour, composed of 1950s-built CIE vehicles, stands on the right, on the far left is one of the distinctive lightweight Park Royal carriages, while Metro-Vickers Co-Co No A13R stands at the platform end.

In the 18 August 1993 picture the rear carriage of the train on the right is one of the very last Park Royals in service - all had gone by the summer of 1994. A General Motors Bo-Bo is alongside it. *Both MHCB*

KILRUSH: Across the broad waters of the Shannon, there used to operate one the best known of all the Irish narrow-gauge railways, the West Clare. The first section opened in 1887, from Ennis, on the Limerick to Athenry 5 ft 3 in gauge line, taking a very roundabout route and eventually terminated at Kilkee, on the Atlantic Coast, and at Kilrush on the Shannon. Desperately inefficient in its early days, and the butt of many jokes, it later pulled itself together and survived long enough to be dieselised in the 1950s. In this picture, taken at Kilrush on 22 September 1960, No F502, one of three Walker 230 hp eight-wheel bogie locomotives delivered in 1955, backs down on to its train, ready to set off for Ennis.

The West Clare system closed down on 31 January 1961, and this is the station on 6 April 1994. The main building is now a private residence and the handsome stone warehouse behind it is now partly occupied by Glynn Marine Supplies, while the harbour, out of sight beyond the right-hand platform, visible in both pictures, has a brand new marina. *R. N. Joanes/MHCB*

ATHENRY, on the Dublin to Galway main line, is the junction of the lines from Limerick and Tuam. No 98, a 'D17' (originally '52') Class Aspinall 4-4-0 built for the GS&WR in 1887, shunts its Sligo to Limerick train at the south end of the station on 30 June 1938 (*above*). This 145-mile cross-country journey took some 7¼ hours; it was, to say the least, a leisurely progress.

In August 1975 (*right*), rebuilt '001' (formerly 'A') Class Co-Co No 032 stands inside the goods shed while shunting the daily Limerick to Sligo freight. *H. C. Casserley/ MHCB*

On 13 August 1993 the pitched roof has gone from the goods shed and redundant track is stacked in front of it, but semaphore signals, the signal box and crossing gates remain. However, although the lines to Limerick and Tuam are still open, no regular traffic, passenger or freight, runs over them today. *MHCB*

GALWAY (1): No 653, a Midland Great Western Railway 2-4-0, built in 1894, shunts the goods yard at galway in September 1959 before taking out a freight for Athlone.

On 10 August 1993 General Motors 2,250 hp Co-Co No 086 prepares to set out with the 22.00 liner train for Dublin. This is the only regular daily freight train out of Galway today, carrying both mail and containers. The track is the same, the telegraph pole is in the same place and the roof of the stone goods shed curves over the second vehicle of both trains. *Both MHCB*

GALWAY (2): At the east end of Galway station in August 1975, looking across Galway Bay to the hills of Clare, the line in the foreground curving towards the camera is all that was left of the Clifden branch. The locomotives are General Motors '141' Class Bo-Bos, the leading one No 156, the other B167, still in the livery it had worn since its introduction in 1966.

At dusk in August 1993 a General Motors '071' Class Co-Co stands under the lamps. Little has changed in 18 years, not even the derelict roofless stone building at the water's edge. *Both MHCB*

CLIFDEN: No 589, a '573' Class 0-6-0 built by the MGWR in 1892, stands beside the water tower on 17 July 1934. The 49-mile branch from Galway to Clifden traversed the heart of Connemara, through some of the most magnificent scenery the West Coast of Ireland has to offer. Sadly there were never sufficient locals nor visitors to pay for the line's upkeep, and it closed ten months after this picture was taken, on 27 April 1935.

Can there be a station site anywhere in the British Isles, abandoned for as long as Clifden, a few months short of 59 years, so untouched by the passage of time? On 10 August 1993 the fine red-brick station house still has its awning and is lived in, and the engine shed has lost its chimneys but is otherwise intact, as is the granite water tower, complete with maker's plate - 'Ross & Walpole, Engineers, Dublin' - and tank, with its gauge showing 'Empty'. *H. C. Casserley/MHCB*

Another view of Clifden station on the same day in July 1934, with a train for Galway about to depart. The locomotive is a former MGWR 0-6-0, GSR No 589, built at Broadstone, Dublin, in 1892. *H. C. Casserley*

LOUGHREA: G613, one of the little 130 hp Deutz diesel-hydraulics, bought by CIE from Germany in 1962, has charge of the single-coach 10.20 to Attymon Junction in August 1975. It was still officially described as a mixed train, though the 'mixed' bit consisted of no more than a parcel delivered to the crossing-keeper at Killmor, beyond the one intermediate station, Dunsandle Halt. Three months later the branch closed.

The station is seemingly intact although derelict on 14 August 1993. Loughrea is on the main Galway to Dublin road and Bus Eireann now provides the town's public transport needs. *Both MHCB*

An earlier scene at Loughrea station on 21 April 1955. MGWR-built 2-4-0 No 656 has charge of the branch mixed train, consisting of a goods van, a six-wheel MGWR-built passenger Brake 3rd, and a modern CIE steel-bodied corridor composite. There were three trains a day in each direction over the 9-mile branch to Attymon Junction, where it connected with the Dublin-Athlone-Athenry-Galway main line. *H. C. Casserley*

ATHLONE: The 08.20 Dublin to Westport stands at Athlone on 29 December 1978. Athlone, in the heart of the Midlands, is the junction of two routes from Dublin, the former MGWR line via Mullingar and the former GS&WR one from Portarlington. No 020 has brought its train from Connolly by way of Mullingar and is about to diverge from the Galway line at Athlone West Junction.

The 11.00 Heuston to Galway, hauled by an '071', passes the now disused station at Athlone on 7 August 1993. With the diversion of all Galway and Westport trains to the Portarlington route, the old MGWR station at Athlone was closed in 1985 and the former GS&WR on the other side of the Shannon, out of passenger use since 1927, was extensively rebuilt and re-opened. *Both MHCB*

MULLINGAR (I): Mullingar No 2 cabin in August 1976. The line from Athlone is to the right of the podium beside the cabin, erected for exchanging the single-line staff - the double-track section through Mullingar station ends here. The rest of the tracks are sidings, used to store rolling-stock which had made its last journey and was waiting to be broken up (see overleaf), some of which is being shunted by Metro-Vickers Co-Co No A4R.

By 2 April 1994 the cabin has gone, as have all the wooden-bodied carriages and wagons, leaving the sidings for the use of the permanent way department. The large gantry with its travelling crane was built by the MGWR in 1923 as the depot for its Morris-Bretland track-relaying train. *Both MHCB*

MULLINGAR (2): A couple of former GS&WR wooden-bodied bogie corridors being broken up at Mullingar in August 1972.

In the second picture is an ancient wooden-bodied bogie carriage at Mullingar on 7 August, 1993. That such relics can still be found here is all due to the Railway Preservation Society of Ireland, which has set up its southern base in the former locomotive shed here. The RPSI has gathered together both fairly modern post-Second World War steel-sided carriages, which have been restored to contemporary CIE green livery and are in occasional passenger use, and much older stock, formerly in departmental use. These, it has to be said, have been acquired in varying states of decay, and this example, a former Waterford, Limerick & Western arc-roofed corridor dating from the 1890s, is in a truly sorry state. It is remarkable that anything from a company that was absorbed by the GS&WR in 1900 should survive at all, but it will take an enormous effort, in both man hours and finances, to save it from complete dereliction. *Both MHCB*

MULLINGAR (3): B132 stands in Mullingar station in August 1972 with a Westport to Dublin Pearse train. The '121' Class Bo-Bo wears the black, white and orange livery introduced in 1961, which was superseded in the early 1970s. *MHCB*

Ten years later (*right*), on 10 April 1982, preserved '101' Class 0-6-0 No 184 stands at the down Sligo platform with an 'Easter Bunny' special.

In the third view, dated 7 August 1993, we see on the left the Athlone line platforms, which now see no regular traffic, and to the right the Sligo line ones. Little, if anything, seems to have changed since 1982, or, indeed, 1972. *Charles Friel/MHCB*

CLAREMORRIS: Aspinall 'D17' 4-4-0 No 98 stands at Claremorris on 29 June 1938 with a Sligo to Limerick train. The first railway to reach Claremorris was that from Dublin and Athlone in 1862. Later that year it was extended to Castlebar and, four years on, to Westport. A third line was the Ballinrobe branch, which was completed in 1892. Claremorris gained a second station in 1894 when the GS&WR line from Tuam arrived. A year later an extension brought this into the MGWR station, while at the same time a fifth and final line, that to Collooney, completed the layout at what had now become an important junction in the West of Ireland. No 98 is immediately south of the station where the two tracks become one and will curve around the south-west end of the town before crossing over the Tuam road and entering the long disused GS&WR station.

At the same spot in August 1993 the Claremorris to Tuam line is still open, but sees no regular traffic, and the Ballinrobe and Collooney lines are closed. Both tracks have been relaid with more substantial rails and chairs some time since 1938, the signal wires and one set of point rodding are still in place, and the tracks are still in use for shunting movements. Claremorris is the nearest station to the shrine of Knock, and pilgrim trains used to converge on the County Clare junction station from all directions, often conveying special ambulance carriages. Although not quite vanished, this traffic is much diminished. *H. C. Casserley/MHCB*

Walking along a few yards we find ourselves at the station, with its plethora of semaphore signals and sidings. Like the town it serves, Claremorris station has changed little over the years, and apart from a fresh coat of paint does not look much different in 1993 from 55 years earlier. *MHCB*

The Claremorris station dog inspects the crossing at the north end of the station. In the platform that rare phenomenon in the 1990s, a branch line train, awaits departure. Of its two carriages, one, the BR Mark I brake/heating van, dates from the 1950s, the Craven standard was built in the early 1960s, while the GM '141' Class locomotive is almost 30 years old. This train runs behind the 13.00 Heuston to Westport - the 16.03 from Claremorris - then forms the 16.17 Manulla Junction to Ballina, arriving there at 16.50. *MHCB*

MALLARANNY: 'D17' Class 4-4-0 No 57 takes water at Mallaranny while working the 11.40 Achill to Westport on 18 July 1934. Mallaranny village is situated most picturesquely on the shores of Clew Bay. The MGWR built a hotel here, overlooking the bay and adjacent to the station, just to the left of the picture. This 26-mile branch was one of the earliest standard-gauge ones to succumb to road competition; it outlived its fellow West of Ireland Clifden branch by two years, being closed in September 1937. Another County Mayo branch, the 7-mile one from Ballina to Killala, had closed in July 1934.

In August 1993 trees and bushes obscure the hills of the Corraun Peninsula, visible in the previous picture. The station buildings, behind the photographer, are more or less intact though much knocked about - a sheep came scurrying out of one on hearing my approach. The hotel lasted much longer, but at the time of my visit that too was empty although seemingly still in good repair and awaiting a new owner. *H. C. Casserley/MHCB*

95

ACHILL: No 57 takes on water while standing on the turntable at Achill on 18 July 1934. The waters of the Atlantic come up to the edge of the goods yard, and beyond is Achill Island itself.

Gorse bushes prevented me from standing in precisely the same spot as Henry Casserley had done 59 years earlier - I got severely spiked as it was - but it can be seen that in August 1993 the station building, visible above the cab of No 57 in the previous picture, is still in existence; it is actually now a hostel, as is the goods shed near the waters edge. *H. C. Casserley/MHCB*

Right The water tower at Achill in 1993. The pipe to which the hose was attached whence No 57 was quenching its thirst can be clearly seen. *MHCB*

BALLYSODARE was the last station before Sligo, 4 miles distant. In this picture, taken on 29 June 1938, Sligo, Leitrim & Northern Counties Railway 0-6-4T *Lissadell* has charge of a mixed train from Enniskillen to Sligo. Between Collooney, 2 miles south of Ballysodare, and Sligo, Dublin to Sligo trains shared the tracks with those of the SL&NCR. This latter railway, some 48 miles in total and completed in November 1882, served a sparsely populated rural area, and always struggled to make ends meet. The division of Ireland in 1922 did nothing for the prosperity of the SL&NCR for its trains now passed through an international frontier at Belcoo, some 11 miles from Enniskillen. However, it kept going, much of its business being in the transfer of cattle to the GNR at the latter town. When the GNR line through Enniskillen closed in 1957, that was the end of the SL&NCR too. Such a poverty-stricken line had to make do with far from up-to-date rolling-stock, as is only too obvious. The fragile-looking *Lissadell* was delivered from Beyer Peacock in 1899, while the six-wheel carriage it is towing was an ancient thing bought second-hand from the GNR in 1936.

With the disappearance of the SL&NCR there was no need for two tracks, the station was closed and the single track now serves neither of the derelict platforms. 12 August 1993. *H. C. Casserley/MHCB*

The Second World War gave a great boost to rail travel in the North, with increased military activity and severe restrictions on private motoring, and the SL&NCR benefited to the extent that it was able to bring into service two new steam engines and a new railcar. The latter was built by Walkers of Wigan and consisted of a power car and trailer, of similar design to some pre-war narrow-gauge vehicles. The lone survivor of the SL&NCR railcar fleet, it was bought by CIE in 1959, renumbered 2509, and performed miscellaneous duties, including driver training. Not surprisingly it was a favourite for Irish Railway Record Society outings, and is seen here at Limerick Junction in August 1973, by which time it had become the last former SL&NCR vehicle in service, although as far as I know it never again carried out any revenue-earning duties. It survives, in derelict condition, in the care of the Great Southern Preservation Society at Mallow. *MHCB*

SLIGO: At the head of a Dublin train on 18 May 1950 is No 539, a big Cusack-designed 'D7' Class 4-4-0, built as No 5 *Croagh Patrick* for the MGWR in 1910, and rebuilt with a large-diameter boiler by the GSR in 1939. In 1947, at the height of the fuel crisis, there was only one train a day from Sligo to Dublin, the 9.30 am, which, with 15 intermediate stops, took 5 hours 50 minutes to cover the 134 miles to Amiens Street. Three years later things had improved, but not by a vast amount.

The 17.40 train to Dublin is standing at the platform on 12 August 1993. The station, which is due for rebuilding, has not changed greatly in 43 years; the bookstall has disappeared, as have various panes of glass in the roof. However, there could hardly be a greater contrast between the elderly, wooden-bodied six-wheel and bogie carriages - what few there were - and the rake of air-conditioned InterCity stock stretching beyond the platform. *H. C. Casserley/MHCB*

The business end of the 17.40 Sligo to Dublin, about to depart with two '121' Class GM 875 hp single-cab Bo-Bos in charge. With nine intermediate stops it will take 3 hours 20 minutes to reach Connolly (formerly Amiens Street) station, almost all the journey over single track. *MHCB*

SLIGO ENGINE SHED: A GM '141' Class Bo-Bo stands outside in August 1977, but by 12 August 1993 the shed has been demolished and the inspection pits filled in - more or less. The water tank still stands, and beside it is an '001' Class Co-Co that has brought in the 05.20 liner train from Dublin North Wall to Sligo Quay. *MHCB*

Donegal and Ulster

STRANORLAR was the headquarters of the County Donegal Railway. Here No 14 *Erne*, a 4-6-4T built by Naysmith Wilson in 1904, stands ready to depart with the 9.58 am to Strabane on 7 August 1930. No 14 was one of the engines that survived the closure of the County Donegal on 31 December 1959, being bought by Dr Cox, but it was eventually broken up at Letterkenny in 1967.

When I arrived at Stranorlar on Friday 20 August 1993 there appeared to be nothing to suggest that there had ever been a substantial railway presence here. There was a Bus Eireann garage and I showed Henry Casserley's picture to the Manager. He told me that some of the buildings had survived the railway closure - indeed, I remembered seeing them in 1977 - but the rebuilding of his garage had wiped them out. The one unmistakable landmark was the distinctive tower of the parish church, across the main road from the site. After disturbing a herd of cows during their elevenses, narrowly avoiding several ditches and staggering through luxuriant nettles, I eventually arrived at the back of a store and satisfied myself that this was where Henry Casserley had stood 63 years earlier.
H. C. Casserley/MHCB

LETTERKENNY (1): County Donegal once boasted two narrow-gauge railways, the County Donegal, jointly owned by the GNR and the NCC, and the independent Londonderry & Lough Swilly. Both served Letterkenny, the CDR entering from the south, passing beneath the L&LSR to terminate on the north side alongside the Lough Swilly; there was a connecting line by the engine sheds. In this view, taken on 17 September 1948, one of the unique L&LSR 4-8-0s, No 12, built by Hudswell Clarke in 1912, and the only eight-coupled narrow-gauge tender engines in the British Isles, stands in front of the shed. The open wagon, just visible in the distance, to the left of the rake of vans, is standing on the connecting line running down to the Donegal.

The August 1977 view is taken from where the 4-8-0 is standing in the previous picture. The stonework of the water tower is just visible on the extreme right, and a grounded carriage body sits amongst the undergrowth next to it, while in the yard that used to be the station are derelict buses and lorries belonging to the Lough Swilly. As the company gradually phased out its railway services, so it replaced them by road ones, and as such it has survived to this day - the company even still calls itself the Londonderry & Lough Swilly Railway Company. *O. H. Prosser/MHCB*

LETTERKENNY (2): Donegal railcar No 16, with a Walker power unit and a GNR Dundalk-built body, dating from 1936, stands in the CDR Letterkenny terminus in May 1957. No 16 had covered 862,347 miles in the company's service when closure came some 2½ years after this picture was taken.

Unlike the L&LSR, the County Donegal put its faith in trains right until the end, then buses and lorries belonging to CIE took over, and the station terminal buildings still serve Bus Eireann. In August 1993 a Galway-bound Van Hool-bodied coach stands outside the former Donegal station, the back of which can be seen beyond the awning in the 1957 view of the railcar. *J. G. Dewing/MHCB*

LETTERKENNY (3): The last Londonderry & Lough Swilly train to North West Donegal leaving Letterkenny on 8 January 1947. The engine is 4-6-0T No 4, built by Andrew Barclay in 1902.

I had not visited Letterkenny since 1977, and when I arrived after a 16-year interval new road layouts completely threw me. The Donegal station building was still there, but all trace of the Lough Swilly seemed to have vanished. Then I found a couple of Lough Swilly bus drivers, whose vehicles were parked alongside some Bus Éireann ones where the County Donegal platforms used to be. They told me that the Swilly depot was now in the new factory estate and studied the pictures I had with me with great interest. Eventually they worked out exactly where I should stand to reproduce the picture of the big 4-6-0 setting out across the level crossing in 1947. I'm sorry if traffic cones dominate the picture, but that's what I found. However, there was some slight consolation in that the round-about immediately beyond them is called Station Roundabout, while the County Donegal terminus can be seen in the left distance. *Author's collection/MHCB*

105

DERRY (VICTORIA ROAD): The County Donegal and the GNR both served Londonderry, their lines running in on either side of the River Foyle from Strabane. Indeed, Derry was at one time served by four railways, two standard gauge and two narrow gauge, each with its own station. This is the County Donegal Victoria Road station on 26 April 1953, with 2-6-4Ts Nos 2 *Blanche* of 1912 and 6 *Columbkille* of 1907 heading the 10.00 to Strabane.

After closure the station buildings survived and for a time the North West of Ireland Railway Society stored a number of County Donegal locomotives, carriages and wagons around the site, and even gave rides in a railcar there. However, despite enlisting the help of Derry City Council the Society had to move out in 1979, and all the rolling stock was transferred to storage at Lord O'Neill's Shanes Castle Railway. The main station building still exists, but the platforms have gone; this was the same view in August 1993. *N. W. Sprinks/MHCB*

Two more County Donegal 2-6-4Ts - Nos 5 *Drumboe* and 4 *Meenglas* - are seen here in the background on the CDR tracks at Strabane on 6 August 1964 amongst the rows of carriages. The line had closed down on the last day of 1959, but the CDR rolling-stock seen in this picture had been bought by an American, Dr Cox, with the intention of shipping it to the USA. In the foreground we see former Great Northern Railway 'U' class 4-4-0 *Meath*, built by Beyer Peacock in 1948 and later renumbered 66 by the Ulster Transport Authority, taking on water while working the 10.15 Derry to Belfast train. *Noel A. Machell*

The second picture shows *Drumboe* and *Meenglas* 13 years later in August 1977. None of Dr Cox's locomotives or carriages ever did cross the Atlantic and, as can be seen, by this date the carriages had been reduced to their underframes, while the locomotives, although still recognisable, were looking very sorry for themselves. They were actually standing in no man's land, between Northern Ireland and the Republic, although the travelling people, whose caravans were parked in the former narrow gauge yard, seemed little concerned. Eventually, as we shall see overleaf, what remained of the locomotives and carriages was rescued. *MHCB*

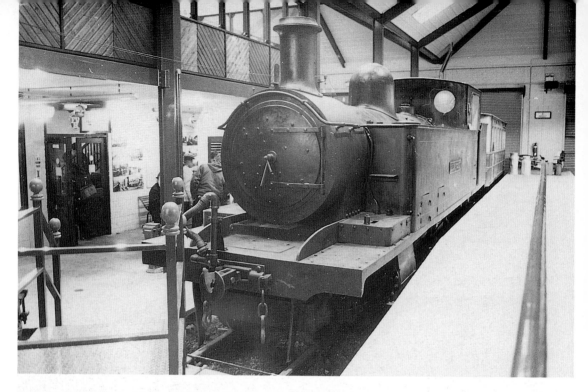

Both the North West of Ireland Railway Society and the City Council were determined that the collection of County Donegal relics should have a permanent home in Derry. A consultant architect was appointed, and a site was selected on what had been the GNR approach to the city, immediately south of the River Foyle Bridge and the site of the former GNR terminus. With help from the European Economic Community a magnificent railway centre, built in traditional red brick, was opened on 6 May 1989. Inside the collection is imaginatively displayed, while outside a 3-foot-gauge line extends for 1,000 metres over the GNR trackbed alongside the river; there are plans to continue this for some 6 miles across the border into County Donegal and the Republic. One of the County Donegal 2-6-4Ts is seen here inside the Foyle Valley Railway Centre. *MHCB*

A view from the driving cab of 41-seater County Donegal railcar No 12, built by the GNR and Walker Bros in 1934, running alongside the River Foyle in March 1992. In 1959, when the County Donegal closed, it was one of the items bought by Dr Cox and was kept under cover, so consequently needed virtually no restoration. No 12 is thus in uniquely original condition. *MHCB*

DERRY (RIVERSIDE): Returning to Derry's four former stations, the only one remaining open for ordinary service in Derry is Riverside. This was the Northern Counties station, serving Belfast York Road by way of Coleraine, Ballymena and Antrim. It was situated on the east bank of the Foyle, downstream from the Foyle Bridge and the site of the County Donegal station. On 1 September 1979 preserved former GS&WR '101' Class 0-6-0 No 186 stands in the station with its Railway Preservation Society of Ireland train of former GNR, GSR and NCC carriages. On the right is a Northern Ireland Railways '80' Class DEMU.

A year later a new station replaced the old Riverside; it was built alongside, even closer to the river. In this picture, taken in April 1992, slightly to the right of the previous one, an NIR '80' Class DEMU stands alongside a rather wet island platform. The pyramid-shaped roofs of the terminal building can be seen in the distance. The train is an Irish Railway Record Society Special from Dublin and Belfast. It had just about stopped raining as we arrived and gradually the skies cleared to give us a brilliantly sunny ride back with wonderful views across the Foyle Estuary to the Donegal hills and, once around Magilligan Point, out across the Atlantic. *Charles Friel/MHCB*

DERRY (FOYLE ROAD) was the Great Northern station at Derry. 'S' Class 4-4-0 No 174 *Carrantuohill* stands ready to depart with the 10.15 to Belfast Great Victoria Street on 13 July 1964.

The GNR line from Belfast to Londonderry closed, despite much protest, on 15 February 1965. This is the car park that occupies the site of the station today. *W. G. Sumner/MHCB*

This more elevated view from the Foyle Bridge of *Carrantuohill* setting off for Belfast allows us to see the buildings on the left, which can also be seen in the 'present' picture. *W. G. Sumner*

DOWNHILL: The NCC main line from Derry to Belfast, having skirted Lough Foyle and cut inland behind Magilligan Point, reaches the sea again at Downhill. In this view, taken some time in the 1930s, a Belfast-bound train is about to enter Downhill Tunnel. Downhill station is in the centre of the picture, the road in the foreground being Bishops Road.

In August 1993 the 14.40 Derry to Belfast passes the site of the station; the platforms remain although all the buildings have gone. William Robb in his *Ulster from the Carriage Window* describes the line here as 'the most dramatic piece of railway travel in Ulster.' *Commercial postcard/MHCB*

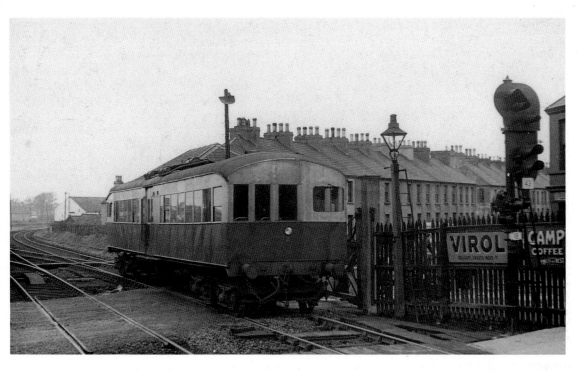

COLERAINE: NCC railcar No 2 enters the station from the Derry direction on 22 April 1948. This far from elegant conveyance was built in 1934, fitted with an aluminium body and two Leyland 125 hp diesel engines. It is shown here in modified form - originally the driving cab was raised as on the celebrated SNCF Picassos.

A three-car '80' Class DEMU arrives from Derry on 19 August 1993. The road has been widened and the original crossing gates replaced by lifting barriers. The trains are passing over the junction of the Portrush branch, which curves to the right, and the Derry main line, which comes in from the left. *H. C. Casserley/MHCB*

PORTRUSH: The premier seaside resort of Northern Ireland, Portrush was also favoured by Belfast businessmen who liked living on the Antrim coast with its wonderful sands and magnificent cliffs, and in the 1930s the NCC built them a special train, the 'North Atlantic Express'. As steam was ending on Northern Irish Railways in the late 1960s the Railway Preservation Society of Ireland, based at Whitehead, on the Belfast to Larne line, was not only acquiring a wonderful collection of locomotives and carriages from both sides of the border, but was also using them whenever it could. One of its longest established and most popular ventures is the 'Portrush Flyer'. On several Saturdays each August enthusiasts and families can relive the excitement of a day out by steam train to the seaside, travelling over the 65 miles from Belfast to Portrush in vintage carriages built by the GNR, GS&WR, GSR, NCC and UTA. In this picture, taken in August 1977, former NCC Derby-built 2-6-4T No 4 pounds up the bank out of Portrush with the returning 'Flyer'.

An '80' Class DEMU is seen at the same location on 19 August 1993. Nothing significant appears to have changed, not even the angle of the lineside telegraph pole. *Both MHCB*

ANTRIM: Situated on the NCC Derry main line, 19¼ miles from Belfast, Antrim was the junction of the GNR branch to Lisburn with the GNR lines from Derry and Dublin to Belfast. On 26 June 1937 No 14, a 'V' Class 0-6-0 built at Derby in 1923 - although the tender is surely a good deal older - enters the station with a goods train from the Derry direction. The last of its Class of three, it was withdrawn in 1954.

Seen from the opposite platform in August 1985, an '80' Class DEMU departs towards Coleraine and Derry. The signal box is a post-war development, and the semaphore signals have been replaced by colour lights, but the station itself has hardly changed. *H. C. Casserley/ MHCB*

The Belfast end of Antrim station in August 1986. The preserved GNR 'S' Class 4-4-0 No 171 *Slieve Gullion* couples up to former NCC Brake 3rd No 91, one of the carriages built for the 'North Atlantic Express', at the head of the RPSI Vintage Train. The signal cabin at this end is, as can be seen, derelict, but semaphore signals are in abundance. The former NCC line to York Road continues straight on, while the GNR branch curves to the right. *MHCB*

DUNGANNON station, looking towards Belfast, on 13 April 1948. Situated on the GNR main line from Belfast to Derry on the opposite side of Lough Neagh from Antrim, this was the junction for the Cookstown branch. No 152, a 'QG' 0-6-0 built by North British in 1903, stands in the branch platform at the head of the 18.15 to Cookstown.

The last section of the Cookstown branch was closed on 4 January 1965, the Derry line following the next month. Looking across this pleasant park on 20 August 1993, there was nothing to indicate that a three-platform station once occupied the site, although behind the camera the big iron bridge that carried the road across the tracks into the town centre remains. Crossing the border some half-hour earlier I was asked by the armed policeman where I was heading. On being told, he remarked: 'What on earth do you want to go there for?', which was a bit unkind; it didn't strike me as being that undistinguished.
H. C. Casserley/MHCB

117

CLONES is a town that is distinctly impressive, and was the meeting point of four branch lines, from Enniskillen, Armagh, Dundalk and Cavan. It was just within the Republic, although so close to the border that the line southwards to Cavan, also within the Republic, actually passed through Northern Ireland. On 18 April 1955 a GNR railcar set, headed by No 616, stands in Clones station. Perhaps even more than the Great Western Railway, the Irish GNR was the leading pioneer of railcars in the British Isles. Following a number of successful cars built at Dundalk in the 1930s, 20 diesel railcars to be fitted with Park Royal bodies and AEC engines, as on the GWR vehicles, were ordered in 1948. No 616 and its companion were two of these.

At the site of Clones station on 19 August 1993 one of the platforms remains, on the left, forming the edge of the car park of Clones Containers and Pressure Vessels, who now occupy the station site. Beside the railcar, and beyond the right-hand end of the modern building, can be glimpsed Clones's concrete roundhouse.
H. C. Casserley/MHCB

This reinforced concrete roundhouse was the most impressive feature at Clones. When the last line to Clones closed in January 1960, the shed survived, for knocking it down would have proved a mammoth undertaking, and it made sense to adapt so solid a structure to industrial use. *MHCB*

Clones's handsome town centre. I had stopped here to ask the driver of the Ulsterbus bound for Enniskillen where the station site was. He explained that this was not his regular run and that he hadn't known Clones in railway days. 'Come and tell me if you find out,' he said, so I did after a young lady in a sweetshop in the square had put me right. *MHCB*

MOHILL: South of Clones GNR trains went through a part of Ireland probably most remote of all from the tourist trail, despite its soft, gentle countryside. They headed for Cavan with its handsome cathedral and its beautiful Harry Clarke stained glass windows, and Belturbet, where they connected with the narrow-gauge Cavan & Leitrim Railway. This is Mohill, with No 10L, a Neilson 2-4-2T dating from 1899, running around its train on 17 May 1950.

On 19 August 1993 most of the buildings to the left of where the engine was posed are still there, but the road has been widened considerably, and the garage extends across where the line used to pass beyond the level crossing. *H. C. Casserley/MHCB*

Swinging the camera around we see that Mohill station, although rather the worse for wear, is still reasonably intact. The Cavan & Leitrim depended for its livelihood chiefly on the Arigna coal mines, and it lasted longer than most narrow-gauge lines, only closing in April 1959 when a power station was built close to the mines, thus rendering the railway redundant. However, at Dromod, where it connected with CIE's Dublin to Sligo main line, a preservation society has relaid some 3-foot-gauge track and acquired rolling-stock from various sources, in Ireland and elsewhere. *MHCB*

Belfast area

LARNE HARBOUR (1): 'WT' 2-6-4T No 4 pulls out of the station with an evening train for Belfast in September 1969. I had arrived at Larne around 6 pm, prior to catching the early morning ferry to Stranraer next day, and was not a little surprised, and absolutely delighted to hear the sound of steam. I dashed down to the station to see No 4 pull in from Belfast, then get ready to return with its train of pre-war corridor carriages; I had never expected to see steam again on an ordinary passenger working within the British Isles. It had ended on CIE some years previously, and on BR in August 1968. The 'WTs' were retained to work spoil trains for motorway construction, which traffic lasted until May 1970. No 4 was the very last serviceable steam engine, being retained for shunting work around York Road through the summer of 1970. It then passed into preservation with the RPSI and can often be seen in its old haunts.

In August 1993 the track layout is much simplified, the goods lines leading to the harbour are gone, and the passenger station has been rebuilt. A P&O ferry dwarfs the two-car 450 Class DEMU. *Both MHCB*

LARNE HARBOUR (2): A three-car MP railcar unit sets off from Larne Harbour for Belfast past a splendid bracket signal of LMS origin in September 1969. The narrow-gauge Ballymena & Larne used to run alongside and to the right of the standard-gauge track before curving away before the latter reached the Town station.

The same view in August 1993 shows a '450' Class DEMU departing. The semaphore signals are gone, and trees and bushes have flourished on both sides of the track, those on the left obscuring the reclaimed inner harbour. *Both MHCB*

BELFAST (YORK ROAD) (1) was one of three termini that served Belfast when I first knew the city in 1959. This had been the Northern Counties Committee headquarters and it served all NCC - by then UTA - trains to Larne, Portrush, Coleraine and Derry. No 95 *The Braid*, a 'W' Class 2-6-0 built at Derby in 1934, is about to pull out with a Londonderry express in about 1948. Although No 95 is clearly of Derby origin, it had no precise English counterpart, and none of the carriages would have looked out of place at Euston or St Pancras, although there are subtle differences between some of the English and Irish vehicles.

Between 1957 and 1962 the Ulster Transport Authority introduced the MP (Multi-Purpose) railcars, conversions from steam stock and fitted with AEC, Leyland, or in one case Rolls Royce, engines. In August 1969 a five-car set stands in the siding between the platforms on the track next to that on which the 'Mogul' is standing in the previous picture. To the left is a pair of former GNR corridor carriages. York Road suffered considerable bomb damage during the Second World War, but nothing much has changed to either the buildings or the track layout between 1948 and 1969.

The third view of York Road, dated 28 August 1976, shows one of the Multi-Purpose railcars, introduced in 1957, again standing on the middle road, and coupled to a rake of containers; the MPs were designed to haul a number of trailers. On the right is a train headed by No 73, a '70' Class diesel-electric railcar introduced in 1966.

Finally we see York Road in August 1993. The back of the terminal buildings are no longer obscured by platforms and awnings, for these are gone and only the track upon which No 73 was standing in the previous picture remains. York Road had by this date been replaced by Yorkgate, built alongside on an embankment to the left of the picture. This was yet another step in the rejuvenation of Belfast's railway system, for the tracks out of the former York Road were in the process of being linked to the new Belfast Central, opened in 1974, by a new elevated line and bridge crossing the River Lagan. *National Railway Museum, York/MHCB/Charles Friel/MHCB*

BELFAST (YORK ROAD) (2): A view from the platform ends at York Road in December 1967. A 'WT' Class 2-6-4T stands outside the locomotive sheds; there were 18 of these engines, built between 1946 and 1950, the tank engine version of the 'W' Class 2-6-0s, and yet another variation on the LMS 2-6-4T theme. Versatile and popular, they hold a unique place in steam locomotive history, for they were the very last steam engines in ordinary service in Ireland and the United Kingdom, the last members being withdrawn in 1971, and, as has already been mentioned, No 4 is preserved in running order by the RPSI.

The second picture is a similar view, taken a little further back into what had been York Road station, in August 1993. *Both MHCB*

127

YORK ROAD SHED, looking towards the station, in September 1969, with No 27 *Lough Erne* taking on water. This was the last 0-6-4T active within these islands, and she and her sister, No 26 *Lough Melvin*, despite their antiquated wheel arrangement, were the last new steam engines to enter service in Ireland, being leased to the Sligo, Leitrim & Northern Counties Railway by their makers, Beyer Peacock, in 1951. Bought by the UTA in 1957, *Lough Erne* was used on shunting duties around Belfast. Withdrawn in 1970, she is now in the care of the RPSI, although is not presently in working order.

A motorway now runs alongside the line out of what was York Road station, obliterating the site of the locomotive depot. This picture was taken in August 1993 from the cab of a DEMU, level with where *Lough Erne* was standing 24 years earlier, approaching Yorkgate, the temporary terminus for Larne line trains while the link to Central station was being completed. The tracks curving away from the site of the old York Road can be seen in the distance. *Both MHCB*

BELFAST (GREAT VICTORIA STREET) (1) was the terminus of the GNR. No 44, one of the little 'PP' Class 4-4-0s designed by Clifford for branch line and secondary passenger work on the GNR in 1896, is about to back down on to a Portadown local in about 1955.

Where No 44 paused, Ulster bus crews' cars are parked on 23 August 1993. The 'Boyne Bridge', which spanned the platforms, remains a prominent feature, and beyond it is the back of the Europa Hotel. *Author's collection/MHCB*

BELFAST (GREAT VICTORIA STREET) (2): The handsome exterior of the station in the late 1950s. *Charles Friel collection*

Yorkgate station, the temporary terminus for Larne line trains while the link to Central station was being completed; August 1993. *MHCB*

Great Victoria Street was replaced by the new Central station in 1974, and a bus station and shopping centre now occupy the site. A statue of two shoppers stands outside; beyond is the Europa Hotel, said to have been the most bombed building in Belfast. 23 August 1993. *MHCB*

BELFAST (GREAT VICTORIA STREET) (3): The 'country' end of the station at sunset in late December 1969.

The same location on 23 August 1993. Not only have all the railway features vanished from where the buses stand, but so have the industrial buildings beyond. On 27 January 1993 the Northern Ireland Economic Development Minster announced that a new Great Victoria Street station would open, hopefully in the spring of 1995. This would be built on part of the site of the original one, alongside the bus station. So once again it will be possible to board a train under the Boyne Bridge and set off for various destinations, some of them never before accessible, for other track developments will allow trains to run direct to the Bangor and Larne lines. *Both MHCB*

BELFAST (QUEEN'S QUAY), something less than a mile from Great Victoria Street on the east bank of the River Lagan, was the terminus of the Belfast & County Down Railway. Here we see 0-6-0 No 14 leaving Queens Quay and accelerating past the depot and sidings towards Ballymaccarret Junction on 5 August 1930. Built, like almost all B&CDR locomotives, by Beyer Peacock of Manchester, in 1904, No 14 was one of only four 0-6-0s owned by the company, and lasted until 1954. The mainstay of the County Down locomotive fleet was the 4-4-2T, built between 1901 and 1945; examples are seen in the sidings on either side of No 14 and its train of six-wheelers.

Queen's Quay closed, like Great Victoria Street, when the Belfast Central Railway was re-opened in 1974 and the new Central station was opened at Mayfields. The Central Railway joined that from Queen's Quay at Ballymaccarret Junction. Although Queen's Quay itself has gone, a maintenance depot and sidings remained until 1994. In this picture, taken on 23 August 1993 from a train on the Central Railway passing the spot where No 14 was photographed 63 years earlier, British Rail Mark II carriages used on the Belfast-Dublin 'Enterprise' stand alongside '80' and '450' Class DEMUs. *H. C. Casserley/MHCB*

BANGOR (1): Until 1950 it was possible to reach a number of destinations in County Down from Queen's Quay, but the lines serving them all closed in that year and since then all that has survived has been the 12-mile-long commuter line to Bangor. No 223, one of the County Down 'Baltic' tanks, stands in Bangor station on 14 May 1950. One of a Class of four, built immediately after the First World War, the 'Baltics' were deceptively impressive-looking machines. They were, in fact, fairly useless, being slower, less powerful and much heavier on coal than the 4-4-2Ts, and were only pressed into service when nothing else was available. All were scrapped in 1956.

An '80' Class DEMU, looking minute compared with the 11 six-wheelers behind No 223, stands ready to depart for Belfast and Lisburn on 23 August 1993. *H. C. Casserley/MHCB*

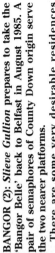

BANGOR (2): *Slieve Gullion* prepares to take the 'Bangor Belle' back to Belfast in August 1985. A pair of semaphores of County Down origin serve the two nearer platforms.

There are some very desirable residences served by the railway all along the shores of the south side of Belfast Lough, and so good is business that the normal service trains run every half hour on weekdays. By August 1993 CTC has replaced the semaphores and the signal box is boarded up. *Both MHCB*

Belfast to Dublin

ADELAIDE station is on the GNR line out of to Belfast. A 'UG' 0-6-0 is passing through the station with a mixed freight on 10 July 1954.

The station is seen in August 1993 from a Belfast-bound express. The old brick and wooden station has been replaced by utilitarian concrete, and in the yard, which used to be the GNR locomotive sheds, stands a '104' Class Bo-Bo diesel-electric. Six of these former 'B' Class locomotives were bought by NIR from CIE in 1986 for use on departmental trains. Although NIR works no freight traffic itself, CIE locomotives haul container trains between Adelaide and the Republic. *W. G. Sumner/MHCB*

DUNDALK (1): The Central signal box with the station beyond was photographed in August 1971. Seen through the arch on the far left is what used to be the paintshop of the GNR works. On the left-hand platform the last Dundalk-built BUT railcar set in service with CIE, headed by No 716N, is about to set off for Drogheda.

The same view in August 1993 shows that little has changed, certainly not the track layout or the semaphore signals. The paintshop has gone, replaced with shrubs and trees, the signal box has been repainted blue, and an '001' Class stands beyond the bridge. *Both MHCB*

DUNDALK (2): South of the station was Square Crossing seen here on 15 May 1950, where Dundalk, Newry & Greenore Railway trains crossed the GNR main line on the level. The DN&GR had been inherited by the British Transport Commission from the LMS, who in turn had taken it over from the LNWR. An agreement in 1933 had resulted it in being worked by the GNR, hence the GNR 'JT' Class 2-4-2T hauling two LNWR-designed vehicles, a van and a six-wheel 3rd, the latter still, remarkably, sporting LNWR livery. The line closed on 31 December 1951, but 'JT' No 93 of 1895 and DN&GR carriage No 1 of 1904 are preserved at the Ulster Transport Museum at Cultra. The train is running through the heart of the GNR works; engines awaiting attention can be seen on the siding on the left.

The works closed officially in 1958, although a number of the buildings remain and have been put to various uses since then, including assembling bubble cars! To the right, behind the metal fence, are parked Bus Eireann vehicles, while on the left the sidings leading into the works have vanished. The buildings beyond them survive, the nearest now ivy-covered. Opposite, the office buildings attached to what was the stores also remain, although ivy has encroached here too and the upper storey has been removed beyond the first four windows. The trackbed of the DN&GR can still be traced. August 1993. *H. C. Casserley/MHCB*

GNR 'VS' Class 4-4-0 No 207 *Boyne* accelerates past the Square Crossing, Dundalk, with the southbound 'Enterprise' in about 1949. The five 'VSs' were the very last, and perhaps the finest, express 4-4-0s built for service anywhere. A three-cylinder simple development of the pre-war 'V' Class compounds - No 84 *Falcon* of this Class is alongside No 207, fresh from overhaul - they were built by Beyer Peacock in 1948. *Author's collection*

HOWTH JUNCTION: On 31 July 1976 a Dublin suburban push-pull comes off the Howth branch and heads towards the city. In the foreground is the Belfast main line, and in the distance are the Dublin Mountains, which provide such a wonderful backdrop to the capital. The area around Howth Junction consists of sprawling housing estates, built since the 1950s as the city has grown and spread along the coast. The next station - the up platform can be seen beyond and to the left of the distant junction signal - is Kilbarrack. The area has become celebrated, or perhaps notorious, as Roddy Doyle's 'Barrytown'. Winner of the Booker Prize, much of the action in one of his films, *The Snapper*, is set in a house in the street running parallel with the railway.

A DART comes off the branch in August 1993. Semaphores and signal box have been swept away and an advanced form of CTC signalling now controls the Dublin suburban area. *Both MHCB*

HOWTH: The last trams in Ireland were the former GNR cars that worked the Hill of Howth line, which was a circular route from Sutton, on the Howth branch, up to the summit then back down to the Howth terminus. Car No 2 is seen alongside the railway terminus on 21 March 1954.

The trams made their last run on 1 October 1959; two have been preserved, but No 2 is no more. Neither, one supposes, is the alternative, equally environmentally friendly adjacent means of transport abandoned by its owner. . . Electric traction now operates the railway, and the tram track is now a footpath, but the signal box **remains.** *N. W. Sprinks/MHCB*

FAIRVIEW: The 17.30 Dublin Connolly to Belfast Central passes Fairview in August 1978. The train is composed of British Rail-built Mark IIb and IIc vehicles dating from 1970 and modified for NIR service. The leading carriage is a brake driving trailer standard, and the train is being propelled by a '101' Class Bo-Bo. The tall building in the distance, above the buffer stops, is Liberty Hall, the headquarters of the Irish Trade Union movement.

A Howth to Bray DART passes Fairview in March 1994. Liberty Hall is still just visible amongst the overhead, while also just visible, at the end of the tracks, are the pitched roofs of Connolly station. *Both MHCB*

INDEX OF LOCATIONS